Successful Leadership and Management in an Aviation Organization – Leader's Notebook

Stephen Taylor Saflin, A.T.P., M.B.A., B.S., A.S.

All rights reserved. No part of this book shall be reproduced or transmitted in any form or by any means, electronic, mechanical, magnetic, photographic including photocopying, recording or by any information storage and retrieval system, without prior written permission of the publisher. No patent liability is assumed with respect to the use of the information contained herein. Although every precaution has been taken in the preparation of this book, the publisher and author assume no responsibility for errors or omissions. Neither is any liability assumed for damages resulting from the use of the information contained herein.

Copyright © 2023 by Stephen Taylor Saflin

ISBN 978-1-4958-1821-9

Printed in the United States of America

About the Author

Stephen "Steve" Taylor Saflin first flew in a controlled manner and under power in an aircraft on 10 June 1976 in a Cessna 152 from the Rostraver Airport in Southwestern Pennsylvania.

Before that:

He was enamored and completely captivated by airplanes as well as flying and attempted flight by testing his own designs made from wood and fabric with marginal success by jumping off roofs and any high terrain.

After that:

He was a United States Army Aviator and received his military Aviator Wings in 1983 after completing training as the honor graduate of his class.

He was in the U.S. military for more than 20-years and flew helicopters and airplanes in support of VIP support, medical evacuation, law enforcement, military operations and intelligence collection missions. He commanded three separate organizations throughout his military career. He was feature in Soldier's Magazine in the June 1987 edition "Had to Fly".

He worked for Cessna Aircraft Company as a demonstration pilot, managed operations, engineering root cause analysis, special mission support aircraft, fuel programs, new aircraft introductions and production test flight for new jet aircraft like the Citation Mustang, CJ series, Bravo, Encore, Excel, Sovereign and Citation X.

He managed the flight and security department for MGM Mirage, operated Gulfstream G-IVSP, G-V, G-450, G-550 and Boeing Business Jets.

He was the Chief Pilot and Director of Operations at ConocoPhillips managing the Part 91 and 125 flight operations, for the company ERJ-135 shuttle operations.

He managed the flight and security departments at Phillips 66 Part 91 operations.

In his career he has been an acceptance test pilot for the military and managed the completion and testing for the RC-12 series aircraft prior to deployment and delivered the aircraft to its operational unit.

He has conducted production test flights on more than one hundred different Citation aircraft and delivered more than 50 to end users.

He has purchased and placed into service eleven new aircraft including the Gulfstream 350, 550, 600 and Boeing Business Jet and also completed the delivery of the green 737-700 NG from Boeing and managed the completion efforts and entry into service.

He has managed organizations with over 200 Aviation team members.

He has flown missions to and in Europe, Africa, Middle East, Russia, China, South America, North America and Central America. The best mission and favorite aircraft was the last one flown!

His favorite mission is being a husband to his wife, Stephanie for more than 34-years, father to Stephen, Seth and Sarah, his favorite son-in-law, Brent, and Grandfather to Ethan, Mason, and Sloan.

Please contact Steve at Stephen.saflin@gmail.com for more information on any topic that requires more discussion to be helpful in your organization.

"We need people that will work to make the environment a better place to be and help us to create a great workplace and a great place to work for our employees. That doesn't happen by itself. It only happens when every individual is aligned to make that happen."

Greg C. Garland, Chairman and CEO of Phillips 66

"The only source of knowledge is experience."

Albert Einstein, 14 March 1879 to 18 April 1955, Theoretical Physicist, during a discussion developing experiments testing theorems for quantum mechanics.

"We stay in the air to keep our ear to the ground."

Sam Walton, Founder, Chairman and CEO of Walmart

"I think public transport is painful. It sucks. Why do you want to get on something with a lot of other people, that doesn't leave where you want it to leave, doesn't start where you want it to start, doesn't end where you want it to end? And it doesn't go all the time."

Elon Musk

During Q&As at the Neural Information Processing Systems Conference in Long Beach, California, in response to an audience question about his take on public transit and urban sprawl

"Since a reference "book" remains the best and most economical method to collect, organize and pass along information, this form will have to do."

Observation

"To be limited by any measure seems to put a ceiling on our business opportunity. To be flexible in our business, I'd like you to build and maintain a fleet of aircraft that meets our business needs so that it is managed and controlled by us. Any other option may be limited when we most need to travel to support our business."

Mr. Terry Lanni, CEO and Chairman MGM Mirage in the initial objective discussion with the new VP of Aviation Operations, 2007

"Quotes and observations from those in the genius class of people should provide a motivator for us, who are vehemently passionate about what we do not only as a Aviation professionals, but as a passion for what we do and how we do it.

How can we make the most time-efficient form of travel more and more efficient? How can we share our passion more passionately?

Spend just a few moments to think about the perfect travel event. If it was simple, got us to where we wanted to go more timely (from departure door to destination door) and it in itself was a pleasant and enjoyable experience it was deemed successful.

If you are able to say this during a review of your travel experience, then I would add that you had a momentously successful mission and experience... and you succeeded in accounting for the millions of details to make it happen just that way!

Please read on and enjoy this perspective of making Aviation happen." **STS**

Dedicated to my wife and children!

The most cherished day of my life was 10 June 1989, then 8 April, 4 April and 18 March...

The countless days away, the missed anniversaries, birthdays, and Christmas'...

I wished that I could re-do that part of Aviation.

Thank you for all your patience and loving support while we were apart and always making up for the lost time when we were together.

Prelude

This book is written for one purpose, to make Aviation Leaders and Managers responsible for aviation operations highly and unquestionably successful by giving them several experiential ideas that have proven effective at leading and managing an Aviation organization. At the very least, it'll provide an experienced perspective that will provide an example of the other way to do it.

Aviation Leaders represent an industry that continues to enjoy enviable safety records, success, provides broad flexibility, builds trust, and demonstrates mission accomplishment credibility.

It also has an implied purpose to provide important information to the senior leader and non-Aviation professional of an organization that has an aviation organization. Just like any challenge or problem, collaboration and input from highly skilled and knowledgeable people dramatically increases the chances of success. The Aviation leader that was selected by a deliberate process of countless interviews, deliberate processes, screenings, testing, and scrutiny and has most likely been brought on board to lead an Aviation organization because of knowledge, aptitude, and experience. When challenges to aviation operations present opportunities for decision – that is exactly what is needed – experience. Philosophical discussions are insightful and help gain participation points, but as the non-Aviation professional, managing an Aviation organization, insist on seeking different perspectives to solve Aviation problems based on experience. Insist on drawing information from people that can share their knowledge based on experience on what worked and what hasn't. Apologies in advance for the faint of heart and super-egos, but an assignment to the C-suite in an organization, doesn't provide the knowledge from an experienced perspective to solve the difficult Aviation challenges – rely on experience and the Aviation professional that can share what works and what doesn't through knowledge gained through experience because they can define what is successful and what isn't. (True members of the Genius class know this.)

At the time of this writing, aviation transportation experienced a growth in high demand never experienced in the history of Aviation.

Requests for aircraft operational support is at an incredibly high demand, and projections are for the demands to continue to grow well into the future. Demands for new aircraft, new organizations for providing support are growing at rates difficult to sustain. Aviation provides a benefit that is invaluable – Time.

We see Aviation growth continue and since it is the fastest way to travel, it is in fact a time machine. No matter how much money one may have, the great equalizer is that we all have about the same amount of available time in our lives. Aviation allows us to use the time we have more efficiently. More and more people have access to affordable air transportation. It is one of the few remaining capabilities that allow us all to enjoy the wonder of using that time the way we want and more importantly.

As social norms continue to expand, decline or change, it is no wonder that we see people change to air travel. The once glamorous and romantic air travel industry is no more for only those that can afford it. It has become a necessity for success at all levels of our society. As globalization continues to breakdown socioeconomic and ethnocentric barriers, air travel is needed to keep and maintain vital face-to-face connections. While virtual meetings are important – nothing takes the place of face-to-face communications. When critical decisions and relationship development is vital – face-to-face communications are the differentiator between success and failure.

There are thousands of reasons why the demand for aviation is increasing and is forecast to continue to increase. Analysts are projecting that the growth in demand for commercial aviation alone will increase from approximately 645 million enplanements in 2022 to 1.32 billion by 2042. The doubling of our current demand will require us to double the infrastructure and support environment.

This manual is the product of experience – over 47-years of it. Leading, managing, organizing and sustaining an aviation organization that is mission focused, operating in a dynamic environment, and continually changing requires a long list of tools and knowledge. Leaders have always capitalized on experience throughout the worlds use of air transportation – aviation is a truly experiential endeavor. To do it and successfully accomplish the mission takes passion, an enthusiastic attitude, above average aptitude, appreciation, fortune, support, blessings, and experience.

Please use this manual for insight, experience and as a foundation for success. In the end, Aviation success is not judged on anything less than 100% of mission accomplishment. A 95% score overall at anything else may have defined success and drew laudatory comments in any other endeavor, but in the practical application of aviation, accomplishing the mission at 95% is synonymous to getting your aircraft and passengers from New York to Imperial Valley, California when your passengers wanted to be in San Diego. Try that once and a potential career will probably be short-lived as an aviation leader. In one singular act of failure of only attaining 95% the objective, the Aviation leader has to recover from a failure that in any other industry would be commended as highly successful.

The daily mission and responsibility in Aviation is to attain 100% of the objectives.

Keep that in mind to prepare the Aviation organization and ultimately push the throttle up. More importantly, smile when other professions claiming success at achieving 95% of their intended endeavors. Just to receive a passing grade in Aviation – 100% is the minimum!

Table of Contents

Chapter One

The Mission Statement – 100% safely, securely getting there efficiently and exceeding the expectations (page 19)

Chapter Two

Safety – 100% Safety, 100% of the Time – No second place for safety awards (page 24)

Chapter Three

People – Building the Aviation Team - The "who's" that bind this wonderful mission, fill in the variables and inevitably make it happen (page 35)

Chapter Four

The Aviation Organization – Recommended organizational structures and people positions (page 56)

Chapter Five

Meetings and Communications- Yes, it still is the primary reason that define failure in an organization (page 62)

Chapter Six

Aircraft Requirements – Everything that it takes… (page 82)

Chapter Seven

Aviation Finance – The Blessing that the Curse (page 89)

Chapter Eight

Interface with the Senior Leaders and Higher Headquarters – You Are Always Educating. (page 100)

Chapter Nine

The Aircraft Acquisition Process – a Deeper Dive into the Strategy and Decision (page 130)

Chapter Ten

Operations – Packaging the Mission for Execution (page 166)

Chapter Eleven

Maintenance – Maintenance, Maintenance, Maintenance and then More Maintenance… (page 172)

Chapter 12

Care and Feeding of the Passengers – Everything that Goes into "Exceeding" the Expectation (page 184)

Chapter 13

Security of the Passengers, Aircraft, Crew and Support Requirements – Security is a Subset of Safety… (page 195)

Chapter 14

Conduct of the Flight – Hang on, This is Going to Cover A Lot of Air (page 197)

Chapter 15

Base of Operations – Hangar, Support Areas, Travel (page 198)

Chapter 16

Assessments and Audits – In Other Words, How Do You know that You're That Good (page 204)

Chapter 17

Records Keeping (page 209)

Chapter 18

Tradition and Progress – Legacy Items and Ideas (page 211)

Chapter 19

Aviation Organizations and Associations (page 215)

Chapter 20

Aviation Envy – Yep, it is real (page 217)

Chapter 21

Recognition and Awards – How to Exceed Your Team's Expectations (If You Have the Right People) (page 223)

Chapter 22

The New Leader's First 90-Days – Assuming Leadership of a New/Different Aviation Organization (page 226)

Chapter One - The Mission Statement

It begins with the mission and the summarized version – the mission statement. The mission statement provides direction, vision, and focus. It is the coalescing point for any discussion and offers immediate focus to the participants of a discussion. It is easy to break the log jam of a discussion on the importance of everything especially if we are discussion time and resource availability. Every Aviation organization is a support organization – an enabler. We fly aircraft to transport high value assets – people and material. If they are on a plane, someone believes that it is worth the time saving to get them there quickly, on-time and above all else – safely. We deliver people to locations where they can get their jobs done – these are normally big jobs, with high monetary value decisions and actions. We deliver materials to locations – FedEx and UPS have made an incredibly successful business by flying materials from one location to another – aggregating the business and making it affordable regardless of the reasons. Suffice it to say that someone thought that it was valuable and having it transported with the most effective and time-saving methods were necessary.

So how does a mission statement coalesce the organization? It does so in several ways. Firstly, anyone can read the mission statement and it should be the most succinct version of telling the story of what you do.

Secondly, it should immediately provide focus to the entire team, especially when discussions about priorities and work objectives are discussed. A simple question is all that is normally needed; how can we accomplish our mission better by doing any proposed action? If we are going to use the Company's resources, shouldn't we begin by prioritizing the use of time and resources with respect to how it will help us accomplish the mission?

How to design and create an organizational mission statement. Since this will be the basis for prioritizing your decisions, it has to be specifically tailored to the desired intent for which the aviation organization is envisioned. Before we go into too much depth discussing the mission statement, we must address who will be required to make the mission happen – the Aviation personality types that will be the teams and individuals that will bring the take the intent of the mission statement, understand its requirements, the definition of its success and take action. Taking action is the point of it all. Successfully accomplishing the Aviation mission will require the strong Aviation personality types suited best for each general type of Aviation organization.

Early in the organization's life span, mission statement definition will certainly be useful in determining the Aviation personality type needed for the best opportunity for successful selection.

The mission statement should state who is going to accomplish the mission, what needs to be accomplished, how it needs to be accomplished and why it needs to be accomplished.

An example of an Aviation organization's mission statement may be broad to include as much of the mission spectrum as possible. Specific missions may require more specific mission statements, but for general purposes a broad example of a mission statement may be:

"The Aviation organization will anticipate, plan and execute safe, secure, reliable Aviation operations, to support the greater organization's objectives, effectively and exceeding the expectations."

One sentence provides the:

"who" – the Aviation organization

"what" – anticipate, plan, and execute safe, secure, reliable Aviation operations.

"why" – to support the greater organization's objectives.

"how' – effectively and exceeding the expectations.

It all seems general and lofty but serves the single purpose of stating what the organization does and it also provides a centerpiece for determining priorities for timing and resourcing.

Once everyone within the organization agrees on the mission statement, it becomes the foundation of what the Aviation organization is expected to provide. Once that is accomplished, the mission statement can continuously be referred to as hundreds of decisions at every level within the organization are made simply by asking, "how does this priority of timing or resourcing support the mission?"

Organizational senior leaders, not only the Aviation leadership team, must fully support the mission as stated to be able to allocate the time, resources, and information to the Aviation organization.

Chapter Two - Safety

Aviation Safety is THE primary stated objective in Aviation on which everything else relies upon. Safety, the act of being safe, is not only stated in the Aviation mission statement, but also implied in every task and assignment. From driving or getting to work, the word "safety" should be implied, "drive to work safely", "climb the stairs "safely", plan the mission "safely", plan food service "safely", taxi out from the ramp "safely", takeoff, climb, cruise, descend, land, taxi, park, shutdown engines, "safely" – every imperative or interrogatory statement should have the action-verb "safely" implied if it is not stated.

If you can't do it safely, then don't do the mission – it is really that easy. If you can't envision a completely safe outcome of the Aviation mission, then don't attempt it.

There are hundreds of great Aviation Safety quotes, some are even made into posters. But at the end of the day, or the end of the mission, if anyone was hurt throughout the conduct of the mission… anticipating, planning, or executing, then the mission was a failure. As the Aviation leader, the imperative is that the mission is conducted safely. The Aviation leader is the unbreakable link in the Aviation Safety Chain! Success and Safety are synonymous, or people are injured or killed.

Failing to maintain a safe Aviation environment on the ground or in the air, means failure in the mission and leading.

When a pilot gets into an aircraft cockpit – the only acceptable attitude is that of being a professional. Someone is already thinking about the last statement… "we'll I don't get paid to fly, therefore I am not a professional." If they said that to begin with, they aren't smart enough to fly aircraft. They certainly aren't humble or respectful of the fact that it takes a professional mindset, with a professional's respect of what is about to happen and live in the Aviation environment.

Early in my military aviation career, in fight school, our flight class had an accident. It was attributed to a mechanical. The sprag clutch on a UH-1H helicopter failed and during a practice low-level autorotation, it pulled the main rotor RPM down to the point where the aircraft could not sustain flight. The result was that 3 people died. They were 50-feet above the landing area, the instructor rolled off the throttle and within seconds the aircraft crashed. A few of us were in the area at the time... it is a scene that you'll never forget. I've seen aircraft crash sites many times since that first one... they are all the final resting place for exceptional pilots. If you fly long enough, you won't be able to fly from point A to B without mentally recalling locations or points on the ground where that location became the abrupt and quick end to a flight and an Aviator's final resting place.

Aviation Safety is a deliberate process. In some form or another, it has been around for a long time – but just like anything else, we learn from accidents and mistakes. Our latest evolution is The Safety Management System (SMS) and like all other safety programs, it is designed to prevent accidents. It is detailed, it is deliberate, it makes us anticipate, plan and execute with Safety as the priority. It isn't perfect, but it is designed to allow us to assess a potentially hazardous situation and take steps to mitigate the hazard. If you are part of an organization that doesn't have a Safety Management System, make it a priority to put one in place immediately. If you belong to an organization that doesn't have or doesn't want a Safety Management System, leave that organization. It'll be a matter of time until someday, someplace will become a final resting place. Ego, complacency, and carelessness, among countless other faults, will cause accidents. Flying into a situation for which the crew and/or aircraft is not prepared for will lead to accidents. Taking shortcuts on the checklist, or the Safety Management System, will lead to accidents.

The Aviation Leader is the Safety Officer! Anyone in Aviation is an Aviation Safety Officer. You can designate an Aviation Safety Officer and that may be the person that helps with the administration but make no mistake – if there are 25-people in the department, you should have 25 Safety Officers that are just as vehement about the adherence to the Safety Manager System and culture.

Use checklists – simple concept, a lot of time training, even in complex airplanes. Checklists are vital. Pilots that believe that their memory or processes are infallible are only fooling themselves. Think of all the things that are 100% and be honest, is human memory one of them? Why not use a checklist? You can't remember 100% of the things, 100% of the time. Thank goodness for placards, checklists, and manuals. The only thing you must do is complete your mission 100% safely – that's the absolute.

Give yourself a goal, you have to make it safe and come home better than you left – easy right, you're flying, doing what you love… that therapy alone makes it a breeze to come home better than you left. But the key here is caution and respect for all the dangers. Your smart, your tough, you are literally on top of the world. But when you are going more than 10 miles an hour, or fall from 10 feet, you're probably going to sustain an injury. The point is, in Aviation terms of speed and altitude, you're frail. You aren't going to survive a crash at the speeds you'll impact something and you aren't going to survive a fall with much intact from the altitudes you'll be flying… you can't breathe very well about 14,000 feet for very long, you're going to have physiological issues at sustained high altitude flight. Let's be frank here, you may be tough, but you're going to have to keep everything in balance to survive… The only thing you must do is complete your mission 100% safely – that's the absolute.

Operating your aircraft depends on maintaining it within the certified operating envelop. Cautions, warnings, and limitations are in the manuals for a reason. They are there to help you envision, with certainty, that if you stay within this envelop, you'll have a successful mission. Stray outside of it and who knows what'll happen. Everyone talks about the safety margins and there has to be a little room for error… that little room for error means that if you hold that line and something unexpected happens, you may have enough time to get back to the safe operating envelope before things start coming apart – the operative word is may. Stall speed for example, is just about as absolute as it gets, go below stall speed under the same conditions as the test pilots and they have demonstrated that the aircraft will stall. There may be some variable, G-loading, temperature, pressure, configuration, CG, etc., that could cause a stall earlier or later. Which is why we calculate approach speeds at 1.3 times Vso. And more experienced pilots add a little more to that speed especially in windy and gusty conditions. The key message here is that you must know, respect and operate within this envelope and you have to know what that is. So, there is another 100% in addition to completing your mission 100% safely, you have to comply with your aircraft's cautions, warnings and limitations!

We talk a lot about safety, safety management systems and all the variables you must do in order to complete your mission 100% safely. How you take that all in is what it is all about – your Situational Awareness and ability to account for all the variables both dynamic and static. If you knew, when where and why you were going to have an accident, wouldn't that be helpful in preventing the accident. You could expect it, be prepared for it, and react to it – or better yet, you could avoid it all together. Your SA helps anticipate, plan and act to prevent an accident. Could be that you notice your airspeed deteriorating in straight and level flight, maybe airframe icing, maybe your aircraft autopilot was interrupted, but the key is, you noticed it, and acted before it became critical because of your SA. Multiply that awareness of each variable by a thousand on a good day and you quickly realize how critical it is to maintain hyper-SA when you're flying. That will help you immensely when the only thing you must do is complete your mission 100% safely – that's the absolute.

We do a task a hundred or hundreds of times, we should get good at it, it should become routine, we should know what we are doing. But that is in a static environment. The Aviation environment is anything but static, it is completely dynamic, so even though you have done something hundreds or thousands of times in Aviation, there is going to be one subtle difference if you're lucky, or one big, unforgiving difference if you're not. Complacency is OK if you are an accountant and you have a delete key or a big eraser. It's OK when you are in the simulator and you can hit the freeze button, go back and do it again. But real life and real flying isn't like that. The mistakes we make that don't kill us, make us learn. But there isn't a second chance to redo the big mistakes. Make a big or fatal mistake and there is no do over, and you'll not be able to meet your objective of completing your mission 100% safely. Complacency and getting behind the aircraft are dangerous. Stay focused and get it right 100% the first time.

Safety Meetings – Have them, have them routinely, have them frequently. Talk about the issues that are recent. Have everyone participate. Take roll. Give people that couldn't be there an opportunity to make up the safety meetings. Do whatever it takes to talk about mistakes, learn from them, put processes in place to make it harder to make mistakes. This is the safety drumbeat, it is the alarm clock that bores into the brain that safety is the important part of what we do. It is the constant reminder that anything less than 100% safe accomplishment of an Aviation mission is a failure. If you have the right people on the Aviation team, they won't want to miss an opportunity that safety is not a choice – it is an absolute. The organizational safety meeting is the basic building block of the Aviation Safety Management System. Ideas are shared, reminders are offered, and lessons are learned the easy way rather than the hard way.

Safety Audits – Conduct them and conduct them routinely. Grade your organization and your team members on how well they live the safety culture that is needed for survival. Have an outsider conduct a safety audit. Have your safety officer conduct them. You'll never know how compliant you are until you take the time to specifically review or audit how well you adhere to your safety principals. A self-imposed safety audit is much, much better than a post-incident safety investigation.

Safety Awards – Have a program to reward and recognize those who contribute to the safety culture. Safety awards can be anything from a safety award given at an annual event dinner held in honor of the recipient to a thank you note that mentions the action of a person that epitomized the safety culture. Reward positive actions when people exercise good judgement and live the organization's safety values and culture.

Safety Seminars and Organization – Safety Officers should attend the Safety courses at USC. The University of Southern California was one of the first and still is one of the premier higher centers of excellence for Aviation Safety knowledge and they have been in place since the 80s and are a premier Aviation Safety Officer producing organization. The NBAA has a great Safety Council, Aviation Safety Officer should attend a seminar annually. Flight Safety Foundation does the same – attend at least one of these seminars every year. There are many opportunities for Aviation Safety Officers and Managers to attend safety specific seminars. All of these organizations focus on providing great discussions, they dive into and pull-apart lessons learned to understand the safety failures and accident causes, and focus the organizations safety program on getting back home 100% of the time, without injury or incident. And that, is an Aviation Safety Management System's and the Aviation Safety Officer's primary focus.

Safety and Risk Management Automated Programs – There are many flight risk assessment programs available that assists and manages risks. Once of the most comprehensive and technically capable systems is VOCUS. It considers more variable and information than I have experienced before and gives the Aviation professional the information to make risk reduction, actionable information available anytime when you have connectivity. These programs are just as vital to the safety management systems as any other program in place.

Chapter Three – The People - Building the Aviation Team

Just to be clear about this, if the right people are on the team, it isn't about leadership directed toward the individual. It is about leading the direction and focusing the team and organization overall. If you have the right team members, all the aviation leader does is provide the environment for the right people to practice their passions.

The Aviation Leader needs to provide four basic components to maintain a high performing Aviation organization (please note that these components are equally vital):

1. Resources to complete the mission – all of the things, including sufficient finances.

2. Training specific to the mission – this encompasses all the fine-tuning training and education specific to the organization's mission and requirements.

3. Time – to complete the mission the right and only way - this is usually one of the hurdles, especially when working with non-Aviation companies, where Aviation is a service provider.

4. Information to do the mission – including the mission statement, briefings, de-briefings, quarterly updates, management of change, after action reports and regular team meetings.

While that sounds deep in thought and easily disputed, it really isn't. The aviation mission really comes down to a few people in the right place making things happen in direct alignment with the intent stated in the aviation organization mission. The idea that a leader has any direct involvement in a specific aviation mission, flight, maintenance, ground, logistics and operational support is utopic. Aviation missions are exercises in small group leadership. A flight, a maintenance action, an operational change, ground support requirements… all need capable people that understand the mission, have the attitude and aptitude to make on the spot, critical decisions. The Aviation team needs these four basic components in order to succeed. The Aviation team member needs to have the Aviation attitude and aptitude when they walk through the door of the Aviation organization and unfortunately, the only influence that the Aviation leader has on those two, individually controlled components, is selecting the right members to be on the team.

Firm believers in any other leadership philosophy normally are limited by what they can accomplish themselves. If a leader had to be consulted and had to approve every decision or help their team adapt to the millions of variables in the aviation environment, they would slow the process down to the point of extreme inefficiency and negate nearly every practical advantage to aviation transportation. A single leader can't be in every cockpit, behind every wrench that needs to be turned, inside each operational decision that needs to be made or every ground support requirement change. Aviation needs smart and self-driven people that know how to act when things are falling apart. They must act with quickly, decisively and through experience. That is the hallmark of a fully functional Aviation team.

Building the aviation team requires a very wholistic evaluation of each of the team members. The first question is "does the team member truly want to be there?" If attitudes are driven by the persons thoughts, then Aviation must be the individual's life's work. Any other personal mindset from the Aviation individual creates a very distant second as far as desirable mindsets.

In the smooth order and function of the Aviation environment, the sum of the individual effort is directly proportional to the mission accomplishment record and level of success. This is hardly a novel approach to any effort that requires the collective sum of individual levels of effort. Any well-functioning team has a greater chance at consistent success rates compared to the marginal or dysfunctional team.

Attitudes are everything. The Aviation team member must possess the attitude that will allow for the individual to thrive and successfully contribute to the organization. Passion is a subset of attitude. Passion is what drive the overall success and the overall attitude allows an individual to thrive in an environment where the passion of the job can be practiced. Pay or compensation driven team members rarely have the stamina or dedication to practice their passion. While compensation is a necessity and a component of the overall success environment, it alone cannot be considered the primary motivator, that self-drive must come from within the individual and be part of their core attitude.

The Aviation leader should look for indicators that determine whether it is passion or pay that drives the individual. When meeting with your Aviation team individually, determine if the passion is the primary motivator, then reward with the appropriate amount of compensation commensurate with their dedication, abilities and skill sets that contribute to accomplishing the mission.

Leaders struggle with this challenge in creating a strong, capable, and consistently successful performing team. Compensation must be determined by assessing the skill, talent, and contributions of the team member, but it cannot be the exclusive motivator. Compensation must be fair and in-line with talent levels. A meritocracy in most cases keep the good employees in place. The best talent will be sought after and compensation levels must be at the industry level, or you may have a challenge maintaining the talent level that you searched for when building the team. In dynamic employment periods where talent is rare and essential, the business case must include salary levels that are commanded by this level of talent. I use the word command intentionally since it is a strong imperative – strong, consistent talent "commands" strong consistent compensation levels. At this level, salaries are warranted. Hourly level pays drives inconsistent levels of performance and attracts the non-passion oriented employee. Hourly level compensation will attract "temporary" team members. Contract and part-time team members can augment the full time Aviation Team, but they should not be counted on to complete the key missions that are the cornerstone of the mission.

It is no doubt one of the key issues that Aviation leaders will have to address throughout their career – making hiring decisions that will affect the team for years and possible decades.

Screening candidates for the attitude and aptitude that fits well into the organization is one of the Aviation managers most critical, mission impacting and long-term decision that they will have to address throughout their career. Finding the people that fit the culture and social environment of the organization are critical. There are no bad hires for an organization, there are just people that fit one organization over another.

To address the best Aviation organizational fit for an individual in aviation, describing the type of organization will provide a foundation determining individual-organizational fit.

Here are the five types of Aviation organizations:

<u>Aviation Financial Focused</u> – very specific mission whereas they are trying to carve out a specific niche of specifically generating revenue through Aviation operations. Airline, charter, and shared-ownership operations are part of this group.

<u>Aviation Key On Efficiency Focused</u> – extremely value and efficiency driven organization, minimal investment in support infrastructure, specific missionized fleet, gets the job done and meets the regulatory standards for training, maintenance and operational costs. Most private operators, principal-owned aircraft and small fleet charter operators are in this group.

<u>Mission Focused</u> – important integrated aviation operation, where reliable, safe, secure mission-capable aviation operations that support the core mission of the organization and is essential to supporting revenue generation or objectives efficiently is the

key metric. Business, government, NGO support operations have operations that would describe this category.

Access Focused – organizations and individuals that have lifestyles and/or business requirements that span broad distances, require the time-savings that Aviation operations provide, not integrated into the business, but essential for business and lifestyle patterns. Principal-driven individual, family and family-group organizations describe this category where Aviation time savings provide a key and tangible benefit to lifestyles and business-support operations.

Discretionary Focused – organizations that may have temporary needs for the travel efficiencies and time-savings that Aviation provides but it may not be integrated into a business, driven by business support or access. The aviation organization is dependent on external affordability and funding. It is a bolt-on/off organization that serves a specific purpose for a non-descript time-period. A company that is starting a new project, needs to move people efficiently until a more affordable and sustainable alternative is available. New companies, timing-dependent requirements, new to Aviation families/individuals, and businesses would fit into this category.

Organization Type	Description	Attributes	Personnel Synergy	Discord
Financial	Airline, Charter	Revenue stream	AP Type 1	AP Type 5
Key On	Principal Owned	Specific Fleet	AP Type 3	AP Type 1
Mission	Integral Ops	Integral support	AP Type 2	AP Type 5
Access	Aviation Reliant	Support lifestyle	AP Type 3, 4	AP Type 1
Discretionary	Flexible Model	Depends on C/B*	AP Type 5	AP Type 3

Organization Type Table (*Compensation and Benefits)

Please note – all the organizations above solidly fit into the types of operator's spectrum. One is not ranked any differently than the others. Since the objective at this point is to determine individual/organization complementary attitudes and aptitudes as well as organizational/individual fit, one-type of organization may be suited better for one-type of person.

Keep in mind that organizations and individuals shift between these differing types in their collective lifespan. The types of organization described above serves several purpose, but for the specific discussion it is discussed for the purpose of establishing the best fit for the type of Aviation Team member and gives the Aviation leader an opportunity to determine better fit of personality types, characteristics and desires, all at a specific point in time when the on-boarding for new a new team member decision is made. The organizational leader should know whether organizational adaptations might occur to anticipate the type of Aviation Team member that will best support its operations through its anticipated changes. An organization anticipating change or involved in an organizational change should delay team member on-boarding until the organization has completed its future design strategy, mission statement or end-state prior to adding new or additional full time team members.

Organizations are just as dynamic as people – they both are changing constantly. We may not be able to anticipate the change in the person over time, but we should be able to predict a change in the organization through the deliberate change management process. As the organization shifts from one type to another, it must remember that it will require a shift in the members of the organization. Both are difficult to anticipate, but the organization is the starting point for the process since it is the organization that will hire individuals and make decisions that will cause itself to change through its own decisions. As the change in the organization occurs, it will ask the individuals to adapt to its change. The individual has the capability, and should, determine if the new adaptation occurring within the organizations fits personal characteristics, traits, skills, talents, lifestyles personal and professional growth opportunities.

Suffice it to say that these observations are from observations of over 2,900 military and civilian Aviation team members over a period of 40-years.

Please note: The following information is not a psychological evaluation. It is a summary my observations; it is what was observed by me and seems to be a successful combination of organization and personality types. This is not indisputable. It is my observations based on my experience and observation over a span of 40-years. It is my opinion that I hope will help Aviation leaders understand and address some of the challenges inherent to leading an Aviation organization.

Aviation Personality Types

Aviation Type 1 – expectations are high and commensurate with the amount of dedication. Strong sense of pay for performance. Extremely dependent on policies and standards to define the personal expectations. Loyalty and dedication are dependent on same from organization. Tendency to be suspicious and non-aligned and breaks away as soon as adversity challenges them.

Aviation Type 2 – camaraderie and team oriented: values belonging to a team and an organization. Leads off with dedication, realistic expectations, is a self-starter, only needs to understand the mission and the intent and will take it from there. Enjoys leveraging experience to solve critical aviation challenges.

Aviation Type 3 – Loves the challenge, the variety of missions, assignments, moving from base to base, team to team, loyalty and dedication are not key drivers, regular base compensation and opportunity to make increase compensation is the key driver at times.

Aviation Type 4 – New hires, just received transition training or a new qualification, new experience level, well-trained and right level of dedication. Needs an opportunity to gain operational and practical experience. May not identify with an organization quickly. Dedicated and driven by opportunity to gain experience, increase in responsibility.

Aviation Type 5 – Enjoys opportunity, likes independence and autonomy, may or may not be completely dedicated or committed, motivated by compensation and opportunity, seems aloof a times and non-engaging. May seem egocentric.

Coaching, Counseling and Talking

Most organizations have periodic performance review processes. While there is no perfect process for one person to assess another and provide a standard, most of them are good – especially the processes that recognize and reward not just on the "what" a team member must accomplish, but "how" they must accomplish it.

The Aviation leader provides the resources, training, time and information needed in order to accomplish the mission, but the individual Aviation Personality Type – the person – must provide the attitude and aptitude. Conduct objective discussion meetings, provide specific, measurable, attainable, realistic, and time-bounded objectives or measures of performance routinely. Coaching is the variable and may help to improve attitudes.

With your team members, follow the general rule of praising in public and discussing shortcomings in private.

Shortcomings are a common denominator, everyone has them. Be honest with your team if they can manage constructive criticism. As a note of caution, the same thing that makes Aviation Personality Types perfect for the safety sensitive roles they perform, makes them self-assured and you'll have to develop relationships to get to the opportunities everyone has to improve.

You'll have some that get it and know what they must do – they are the team members that are the most valuable. When you find them, do whatever you can to keep them. If you can find a way to clone them, take advantage of it. You can conquer any objective with them. They are the backbone of the organization. They'll literally take the mission and run with it. They do it right always. They need very little coaching and are perfectly suited to the mission.

You'll have some team members that are in the middle. Normally this is the 50-60% of the people in the middle. Aviation leaders will find most of their time spent with this group. They are great people but may need a little more coaching and care to get them moving in the right direction, but once they get it, they are off and running with your most-valuable team members.

You'll also have the 20% that are easily influenced. They can go either way, so the key is to identify them early on, get them onboard the productive side. Don't despair, this group wants to do the right thing. Even if they seem to get going on the wrong path, they truly want to do the right thing so all they may need is a reason that resonates with them personally. The key is to reward them for positive actions and behaviors early so that they get a clue early on those good actions, both in the "what" and "how" categories. Coaching and counselling are a must. You may ask what the difference is – Coaching is the informative, frequent, not always written, idea-sharing discussions that happen spontaneously or deliberately. But since this segment of the Aviation organization has the tendency to develop more negative traits, more deliberate counseling sessions may be needed. The counseling session should be scheduled, planned, and always summarized in writing. These counseling summaries will prove to be vital if the team member becomes more unproductive to the organization and the accomplishment of the mission. Written counseling statements are the way to share the information with the Human Resources team, including the attorneys that may have to help defend against claims against the company, including government led organizations.

Caution - The faint of heart and sensitive types, and self-identified saboteur types may not want to read this next paragraph – in-fact, I can already predict their rebuttal to the paragraph written that discusses this type of person. They'll be loud, irrational, focused entirely upon what is wrong with the rest of the organization, etc. They are truly the type that is not happy with any or all aspects of their lives, have a chemical dependency or just not suited for Aviation. They are the types that can't define what makes them happy and they hope that they'll know it when they see it. To this type, there is something wrong with everyone else that is in a leadership position. They are the types that when you read their comments, or hear them speak about something they don't like, you would normally dismiss them as "one of those". Because they truly are "one of those." Go easy on them though, spare yourself the agony. The Aviation leader will not be able to "repatriate" them. The best you'll do is marginalize their effects on the organization and that will take time away from the team members that really deserve it.

Aviation leaders must be on the lookout for the saboteurs. And they are easy to spot. They'll usually not be team focused, but they need a following or an audience. These are fortunately rare, but this personality type exists, in every organization, not just the Aviation organization; however, the Aviation organization seems to provide the most fertile environment for the saboteur to survive. Because the Aviation organization is truly built upon small-team leadership, the saboteur will use the small team influence to develop their audience, and provide a steady and effective, constant negative influence within the organization.

The saboteur is defined by the type of person that will either overtly or discreetly work against the leadership and tarnish the organization; they'll bring so much heavy baggage along with them that they are counterproductive to the health of the organization. Everything from substance dependence, basic personality flaws and personal problems create this Aviation Personality Type. The problems that they generate truly outweigh the benefits they provide. They may seem invaluable, but experience has shown that it is much easier to help them out of the Aviation organization and find an Aviation Personality Type better suited for the organization.

The saboteur's methods include undermining the leadership team, negatively critiquing policies and procedures either overtly or discreetly, having negative opinions toward some or every aspect of the organization. The saboteur can be very charismatic, self-confident, capable and generally very good at what they do. If they are in the organization before other team members are brought on board, they may have the advantage of seniority – which can have a multiplying effect on their effectiveness. As a word of caution, this personality type normally is not rehabilitative. The Aviation leader and leadership team needs to identify this personality type quickly and work with them to help them move on. Many big companies that are not Aviation centric may have difficulty understanding how critical it is, but as a note to a Human Resources business partner or senior management member, if the Aviation leader comes to you and needs your assistance helping this person move on – do whatever you can to assist. This personality type is truly that one person that creates most of the issues within the Aviation organization.

If you identify a saboteur, move them on and out of the Aviation organization as soon as possible. Just to provide clarity, these are not the people that offer better ideas for doing things within the organization. They are not the personality types that may occasionally disagree with policies, procedures or operational standards and try to suggest or offer assistance through experienced based knowledge to help solve problems. They are not the problem solvers. They may be the type that is aware that what they are doing is wrong and they'll modulate their behavior to fall in to acceptable boundaries when someone is watching. This doubles the impact. One, they knew something was wrong and two, they knew enough not to do it when someone was watching. These are people that will disagree with anyone or anything just because they feel that they must disagree. And when they find a topic that seems to have sensitivities within the organization, they will exploit it for all they can. As a word of caution, these are not the occasional dissenter that would like to improve the organization. They are not the personality that is having a bad day. They are the type of personality that looks for reasons to have a bad day. If something is running smoothly, they have to be the one personality type that will work at it to find something negative. Simply put this type firmly believes that they must denigrate others within the organization to make themselves look or feel better. The best course of action is to move this type along as soon as possible.

Finding the right people to fit the Aviation organization is easier said than done, especially when the aviation personality types are as closely aligned. Reading through the Aviation personality types lends itself to appreciating the level of detail that must be discerned in order to accurately select the correct Aviation type personality for the type of aviation organization.

All Aviation personality types are extremely smart, passionate about their careers and self-motivated but pairing the two requires an understanding of the subtle differences. One final thought, be wary of team members that are compensation focused, not saying that this is extraordinary but if everything is about compensation then nothing is about professionalism. Aviation professionals should have the attitude to prove their abilities and then the reward follows, not the other way around. There are many examples of Aviation professionals that do the job without focusing on the reward, look for that professional and then make sure that they are rewarded appropriately.

Bottom-line when it comes to people – Aviation is a profession, professionals do the right thing when no one is watching, professionals set the example and they know their own path and limitations. They are most valuable players on the Aviation team are the types that lift everyone with their skills, talents, and abilities. They are the ones that earn the phrase, "it wouldn't be our team without them." There are very few professions that have to operate isolated, with only the crew and passengers, in a hostile environment where mistakes cost lives. Aviation professionals have to be viewed in the wholistic sense that they have the attitude and aptitude to take on the challenges that may affect their mission and part of the attitude and aptitude of being trustworthy – doing the right thing when no one is watching or coaching, exercising perfect judgement and timing – tough to stop everything when you're at 47,000 feet over the north Atlantic at night – quick action and the correct action can mean life or death. The Aviation leader should always be observant and look for capability limitations with their team. Pairing a new Pilot in Command to a difficult mission with new flight crew does nothing more than rely on hope and good fortune for the success of the mission. An Aviation leader needs to understand the capabilities and limitations of their Aviation team. Frequent interaction in the operating environment tells an Aviation leader many things about their team and knowing that is essential. Observe all activities, maintenance, operations planning, crew scheduling, flight operations, ground support operations. See the team in action. Stop in and see your team at the end of the day and after a long week, observe your team when they are stressed the most. Look for opportunities to see your team after that long day, long maintenance event where overtime was needed, after a long week of flying, international time-zone changes, different languages, different food… all are stressful and it is during those times, when individual compensation mechanisms are impaired – that is when you'll see the true person and can accurately measure their capabilities.

If your good Aviation team members make mistakes that are recoverable, support them entirely. As discussed before, the Aviation environment is led by small team leaders, especially when away and flying a mission. Your Captains and Pilots-in-Command are your leaders away from home. The Aviation leader can't be in every cockpit, or cabin, or operations room, or working on every maintenance action. If and when mistakes are made that are recoverable, use it as a coaching opportunity and above all support your team. Since they were selected for those roles with incredible responsibility, they need to always know that they will be supported if everything doesn't go according to plan. Recoverable mistakes are those mistakes where no one was injured, nothing was damaged beyond repair and the mission was completed by fast acting leaders that filled the need to make decisions and get the job done with minimal delay or disruption. Unrecoverable mistakes which can happen, are those mistakes like running out of fuel because of poor planning, intentionally defrauding the organization, signing off a maintenance action that wasn't completed, intentionally falsifying a record or document… these are level of severity that will most likely not be recoverable from by coaching.

Support your Captains, flight crews, maintenance crews, operations team, Aviation support team and away teams always when they are working hard to do the right thing even when no one is watching. They need to know that the Aviation leader will support them in those less severe and recoverable mistake situations.

Chapter Four - The Aviation Organization – Recommended Structures and People Positions

The Aviation organization is standard throughout the organization type and the type of organization that it belongs. The key point for the non-Aviation organization is that the Aviation organization should be placed in the organization's hierarchy close to the entity in which it supports the most (think mission statement and mission agreement) or in the financial hierarchy structure. The supported organization is generally easy to align – whoever uses the Aviation organization to support its mission should be the organization in which the Aviation organization reports. Another way is based on complexity and spending levels. Aviation is an expensive organization. If it assigned to an organization that has little in common with complexities or spending levels, it will be difficult to create a network where the needs of the Aviation organization (time, resourcing, information) are met consistently. It can work but normally that hierarchical structure is simply creating a step in a process that isn't needed. Non-Aviation organizations do this for a variety of reasons; optics or just not knowing where they belong. From personal experience, the best organizational reporting structure is reporting directly to the organization most supported, or from a complexity or financial perspective works best and is least awkward. Reporting structures where the Aviation organization reports to the senior leader where the Aviation budget is 50% more of the total budget is awkward or if the taskings are just a pass-through from the true supported organization. For clarity, the supported organization is the organization that tasks the Aviation organization with 50% or more of its mission assignments.

Think of how awkward this is during budget planning where the Aviation organization has 50% of the hierarchical organization's budget, example:

Senior Organizational Department	$50,000,000.00 /year
subordinate section A	$6,000,000.00 /year
subordinate section B	$9,000,000.00 /year
subordinate section C	$9,000,000.00 /year
Aviation organization	$26,000,000.00 /year

This example demonstrates that the complexity of the Aviation organization and their budget is on par with the senior leader of the department in which the Aviation department reports. It begs the question from a resourcing complexity standpoint of why isn't the Aviation leader on par with the senior leader to which the Aviation leader is assigned to support. Or when budgeting time comes and the other department leaders are in the room and see the budget categories and expense amounts needed, at the very least it creates some interesting break room conversations especially when reductions are required.

The other example supported organization. The Aviation organization should report to the organization that assigns more than 50% of the missions. Any other arrangement creates a pass-through tasking.

The two points here are that in each example, 50% of the taskings, or 50% of the budget, unless the reporting structure and peer group truly understands the value intrinsic to the supported organization, it creates a "why is that needed" situation and if the value is truly understood the role of the Aviation leader changes from solving Aviation challenges to justifying the aviation mission to people that don't use it and don't understand the value.

Let's assume that in every organization there is a deliberate decision and not just an afterthought to place the Aviation organization at the right structure level; either managing like amounts of budget and not more than 50% of the greater organizations budget and it is aligned from where more than 50% of the taskings originate. What Next? Here's the organizational standard:

Aviation Leader – Vice President of Aviation and Travel, Aviation Director, Chief of Aviation are typical titles recognized and reports to the Senior Vice President, Executive Vice

President, or Chief Executive Officer. Responsible for everything that happens or fails to happen in the Aviation organization and is also the implied Chief of Aviation Safety.

Aviation Operations Manager – typical title and is responsible for managing the overall mission requirements and coordinating everything that goes into anticipating, planning, and executing the Aviation mission safely, securely, and efficiently and reports the Aviation leader.

Aviation Chief of Maintenance – typical title and is responsible for aircraft readiness and reliability, maintaining the aircraft in a "Like-New" condition and have a 100% mission reliability and reports to the Aviation leader.

Chief Pilot(s) – typical title and is responsible for pilot readiness and making sure that aircraft can be crewed with trained, ready, professional, proficient and knowledgeable pilots 24/7. Normally a Chief Pilot is assigned to each aircraft model or type and reports to the Aviation leader.

Chief of Cabin Crew – Chief Flight Attendant, Chief Flight Service Coordinator, Chief Flight Technician is responsible for cabin crew readiness and making sure that aircraft can be crewed with trained, ready, professional, proficient and knowledgeable cabin crew members 24/7 and reports to the Aviation leader.

Aviation Safety Officer – Safety Manager and Safety Officer are typical titles. Responsible for assisting the Aviation leader in managing and maintaining the Aviation Safety Program and Aviation Safety Management System (SMS). Reports directly to the Aviation Leader.

Aviation Facilities Manager – Responsible for maintaining buildings, grounds, hangars, ramps, fixed-base operations type support, food services, airport services, support vehicles, lighting, support operations 24/7. Reports to the Aviation leader.

Aviation Finance and Administrative Manager – Responsible for maintaining the Aviation ledger, supporting the budget development, managing invoices and payments, coordinating office administrative support, Human Resource requirements, records keeping and schedule coordination. Reports to the Aviation leader.

Travel Manager – supports all travel services within to support the company. Responsible for Part 121/125 commercial air support ticketing, hotels, rental cars, and coordination. Reports to the Aviation leader.

The Aviation Operations Specialists, Aviation Maintenance Technicians, Pilots, Cabin Crewmembers, Aviation Facility Staff, Line Service Technicians, Administrative Staff assigned to the Aviation department leaders. Size of the organization depends on the scope of the mission.

Chapter Five - Meetings and Communications

Information is a vital component that the Aviation leader must provide to the organization. There are multiple levels of continuous communication:

1. Supported Organization Communication – this type of communication is necessary for the senior leader group responsible for the Aviation organization. The flow of communication to this level within the organization provides information and request information. It covers all parameters of communication. The old adage, "bad news doesn't get any better with age" is an easy way to say, share the good but especially the bad with the organization leadership. The information provided by the Aviation organization should cover everything from Status Reports to Key Performance Indicators. Here are the different types and timing of the critical

communications that the Aviation leader should provide to the organization:

a. Weekly Updates – provided weekly and covers these four basic areas:
   i. People – any key issues that affect the Aviation team's people. Medicals, safety, promotions, difficult team member counseling summaries, and changes in status.
   ii. Security and Safety – any issues that are on the safety and security watch list, i.e., changes to security postures, security concerns, facility security issues, safety issues and meeting recaps, any pertinent safety concerns or actions pending.
   iii. Operations – a quick summary of the week ahead or last week summary of mission details (number of flights, new areas, key Executive support missions, non-routine operations, and concerns), maintenance downtime, availability rates, outside support requirements and critical external support needs.

      iv. Logistics – large spend forecasts, critical support requirements, major parts, or inspections – generally anything that supports the mission with parts, outside services and is critical to mission support should be addressed.

      v. Communications – Leader availability (out of the office time, who has delegation of authority in your absence), team meeting summaries, reports or any staff actions that require Aviation input. This is a great section that covers the "all other requirements for effective communications" block to check.

b. Status Reports – This periodic report can be tailored based on the organization. Submitting this report on either a monthly or quarterly basis suffices depending on the Operations Tempo (OPTEMP) – the speed in which things happen within the organization). A single aircraft department may only need a quarterly Status Report if it only flies a few hundred routine missions, but a flight operation with a hundred aircraft may complete a bi-monthly Status Report. Since this is a time-based report and the timing should be routine. If monthly, the report may be published the first Monday of the month, or as appropriate. Whatever the timeframe it should be a routine report that comes out on the same periodic schedule. Status reports normally cover the Aviation organization's Key Performance Indicators. Normal – Routine Status Reports normally contain the following topic areas:

i. Flying Hour Program (FHP) details – number of total hours flown for the reporting period, number flown by aircraft (organic and external), broken down by each aircraft times and then totals.

ii. Flight Activity Forecast - Next period (monthly or two-week period) flight activity summary. Could be a by mission summary that includes date, destination, supported organization, destinations and expected flight hours.

iii. Maintenance Down Time Forecast – what aircraft will be unavailable for mission support during the forecast period. Schedule maintenance events just as you would flight activities to account for aircraft in maintenance and not mission capable. The Aircraft Operations Rate data should also be included in this section of the status report. Operational rate is simply the percentage of time an aircraft was available to support flight missions compared to the time that it was not.

iv. Financial Data – Operating Budget Status - What is the total budget, how much have you spent and a relative rating of if you are on target to meet the budget for the budget period. List the following information so that you have transparency and a quick reference of the status of your operating budget:
   1. List your total budget.
   2. List the amount of the budget you have consumed through the end

of the reporting period – year to date information.

    a. e.g., Annual Budget $30.0 MM, YTD for the first six-months - $15.0 mm

3. List the fully burdened cost per flying hour year to date: simple calculation of year-to-date total budget spent divided by number of flight hours. $15.0 MM TYD budget consumption divided by year to date hours flown – YTD budget spent = s, Total flying hours YTD – h, to yield the fully burdened cost per flying hour – (CPH):

Where:

s = 15,000,000.00 US Dollars,

h = 1,500 flying hours,

CPH = s/h. e.g., $15,000,000.00 / 1,500 hours = $10,000.00/flying hour.

If a company uses charter or shared aircraft to augment the owned or organic fleet, then complete this calculation separately but in the same manner. This will allow you to continually compare the most efficient costs for each aircraft flown.

v. Fuel Cost and Consumption Data – Fuel costs account for a large part of your variable cost calculations. Fuel usage and cost data provides a readily available status of how you are using key resources, i.e., aviation fuel. This data normally is tracked through invoices. The accountability process would account for all the same types of fuel purchases; Avgas, Jet fuel, motor fuel, etc., and account for the total used for the reporting time period and monitor what was the estimated usage, actual usage, estimated or budgeted cost and actual cost. We would normally use a flight hour as our basic unit of resource cost, but since every type of operation consumes fuel, APU run time, block time or engine ground run operations must be factored into the equation.

vi. Estimates and Projections – a fundamental regression analysis will allow for a reasonable accurate forecast or projection of resource usage. A 30-day or consistently periodic forecast of flight activities (item ii above) based on schedule and historical data yields an accurate periodic projection to forecast resource consumption and identify shortfalls or excesses. Finance Officers are notorious for asking for projections and this will help the Aviation Manager provide data-driven forecasts and projections and monitor long-term conditions that may affect the budget and flying hour program during budgeting period. A note of caution here is that every organization has it financial tolerance spectrum – which is a polite way of saying the amount of latitude that an organization has for meeting budget requirements. This is specific to each organization. The Aviation Manager must be acutely aware of that tolerance spectrum. And a great question to ask if you are new to the organization or during key leadership changes (your supervisor, the Chief Finance Officer, and Chief Executive Officer).

vii. Cycle times – landings and takeoffs and the time in-between during flight accounts for the aircraft cycle time.

For example, 3:1 would be three flight hours for each takeoff and landing cycle. The higher the ratio, the more efficient the utilization of resources.

Less fuel is proportionately used, less pressurization cycles, less brake wear, less tire wear, less flexing, bending, and jarring… that all factors into wear and tear. Wear and tear directly affect the aircraft maintenance costs. The lower the ratio, the higher the wear and tear. Predicting cycle time ratios accurately in the budgeting process will make for more accurate budget predictions. Put the actual cycle time of the fleet into the status report so that resource utilization can be predicted with greater accuracy.

viii. Headcount – This is the Aviation organization's most important aspect. For emphasis, the people that are part of and have met the mission month after month and year after year are the most important aspect of the Aviation organization. And at some point, in the organization's design there may have been a deliberate process to have enough people on the Aviation team to do the job with consistently predictable exceptional results. After leadership changes, mission changes and countless other changes including leadership philosophies, the numbers shift from what was required to the current state. Since change is a normal human condition, keeping up with headcount is vital. The Aviation Status Report is a good reminder of how many people that you have and how many that you need. It would normally be listed in columns of people, departments, number authorized and actual numbers. There is a science to this prediction, and we'll cover that in subsequent chapters.

ix. Activities Summary – Keep a one-line summary of key actions, things that must happen, resources required or mission vital requirements. This would be the final and key section of the Aviation Status Report and serve as an update that if these key items could undermine mission success.

c. Quarterly Updates – These are another version of the periodic update where the primary audience is the Aviation Team, but it should be shared with the senior leadership group too so that they can reinforce or assist with the messaging. The objective of this update is to give the Aviation team a recap of the past and a glimpse into the future. It has data that can be used to show the "state of the organization" and allow each person on the team to answer, "where have we been and where are we going." This report should be written for the Aviation team as the audience and provide a summary of some of the routine questions that the team asks frequently. Some of the areas to cover might include:

    i. Mission Statement Recap – State the mission and whenever possible reinforce the mission statement. It is the reason that the team exists and helps each member fill in the ultimate question for all team members in Aviation – where exactly do I fit in to this mission? No matter how difficult this sounds, there will be someone on the Aviation team that wants to know the answer to the proverbial meaning of life. The ones that are persistent and ask the question repeatedly to ask it for several reasons. To give them the benefit of doubt, get all of the folks that ask the question together for a long, happy, hour discussion, (please notice that there is a comma between happy and hour so this doesn't turn into a happy hour discussion where no one will remember anything), to break the mission statement down into the stated and implied mission. Use any formal meeting time to restate the mission. It is the reason the team exists and important for each team member to answer where they fit in.

ii. Agenda – list your key agenda items. Helps them anticipate time requirements and keeps groaning to a minimum.

iii. Program or "Flavor" or the Quarter – These are the key topics, initiatives, changes, additions, hot-buttons, etc. This is the place reserved in the Quarterly briefing for the "new" ideas to be briefed, discussed and where inevitably the team will cheer wildly. New performance review programs, compensation programs, efficiency strategies, overviews of business changes and anything that gives the Aviation team the important "look into the future." Remember this slogan, there are no bad ideas, just bad implementation strategies. Aviation leaders have input on the implementation strategy, so help, don't hinder.

iv. Overall, Company Performance Summary – Use the Quarterly Earnings Statement to summarize the company's performance. Compare the same data from a comparable point in time to the most recent – again, this allows the Aviation team to determine the position of the company. Business Unit Earning's Pre-tax is a good start. Break down the earnings report by unit and compare it to the selected time frame. The bottom line should be the company's bottom line, was it successful in generating revenue. Ultimately, the team should be able to gauge the overall stability of the company and help them make career decisions. At the very least, team members should be able to ascertain whether it is a good time to ask for salary increases, remodeling of the breakroom or ask for new equipment.

v. Aviation Team Mission Statistics – Review what you have done since the last update:
   1. Budget comparison and targets – Look at planned vs. actual for the time frame, cover areas that are Aviation controllable, help team members understand where they can make a difference.
   2. Flying hours planned vs. targets.
   3. Maintenance capability and operational rates – required to meet the mission vs. actual.
   4. Individual duty time statistics – the average flight hours, on duty days, remain overnight, time off-duty statistics -= these numbers help each team member know where they are in the hierarchy of support.
vi. Special information and program discussions: performance review updates, Company programs, safety information, and pertinent details about the direction of the Company

Subordinate Leader Meetings

Meet frequently with subordinate leaders. The Chief Pilots, Operations Officer, Safety Officer, Facilities Manager, Maintenance Chief, Finance Manager, Travel Manager, Human Resources, Legal, Procurement and Administrative Manager all have the key insights about the critical issues. Make time to talk to them routinely as a group and individually.

Schedule Monday Morning Meetings to discuss the week ahead.

Schedule Staff meetings once or twice a month to get the team together for more in-depth discussions about the challenges and opportunities.

Schedule one on one meetings bi-weekly or more often if needed with all subordinate leaders.

Find the informal leaders within the organization, the quiet-confident team members that get the job done and have a following out of respect for their abilities. These are the informal leaders that should be given the opportunity to discuss the issues. They may not be in official leadership positions, but they are the ones that are observant, deliberate and truly want to see the team do well.

Chapter Six - Aircraft Requirements

All aircraft designs are compromises. Modern aircraft are safe, efficient and they are in effect a time machine. They must be designed to operate in a very strict environment of physical laws and certification requirements. One of the eyebrow raising comments heard from non-Aviators is "thinking outside the box". That statement should make any aviation professional cringe since the "boxes" where we operate are tight and the very defined reality within Aviation that aren't compatible with wild creativity.

Science fiction has the limitless boundaries to describe incredible machines that can do fantastic things but living in an environment that has very defined realities shrinks the box in which Aviation operates. In our earth's atmosphere, lift, weight, thrust and drag are defined by mathematical equations that give only one right answer. One side of the equation can't be changed without affecting the other.

A non-Aviator speaks in lofty goals. An aeronautical design engineer once told me that if an aircraft was designed to fly around the world twice at the speed of light and carry an infinite payload, someone that has not experienced critical design theory in aeronautics would want to go around three times without refueling at twice the speed of light and carry an infinite amount of weight plus one!

It is a nice fantasy and I hope that some genius can solve that equation… it would make the Aviation professionals life a lot easier.

Since we haven't determined that solution at this point, we'll have to make do.

How do we determine the right solution? Let's go back to the mission; how much, how far, how capable is a good place to start. Start with defining the normal mission profile in a realistic sense. Keep in mind that this is a time issue as well as a geographic issue. Aircraft are designed to fly direct and fast, so any diminution of that aspect takes away the advantage of flight.

Commercial air travel can sometimes be a good example of how we make a difficult case as to why time is vital to the solution set. A flight from a large west coast city to a smaller Midwest city requires changing planes (my favorite example of the hub and spoke system that is typically used in any distribution system). Depart fly 600 miles at 500 miles per hour… land to change planes… plane is delayed, next flight out is the next day… cover the remaining 400 miles at 500 miles per hour – we just traveled 1,000 miles in 18 hours or 55 miles per hour. (See a very smart persons quote at the beginning of this book to put it into perspective.) So we've spent a lot of money, TIME, and effort to make traveling 1,000 miles at the same rate as the most basic automobile. Great example of how defining the requirement is vital in Aviation.

How do we begin to optimize the solution? Begin with defining the normal parameters.

Normal mission parameters

1. Location pairs – what geographic points on the earth are you trying to connect? We define this as city pairs, airport pairs or locational pairs or the point A and point B. If there is historical data, start there. For new operations, what is the business case or business units. There can be a few, tens, hundreds, or thousands – connecting the business centric points is a study in geography. The geographic points will define the normal distance that needs to be served to effectively support the mission requirements.

2. Airports (landing and takeoff operating space) is another key point in determining the geographic constraints. This usually will help define the performance requirements of the aircraft. As an example, to this point, two geographic locations may be distant and need a large aircraft, that carries enough fuel weight to reach the destination non-stop. Operational performance may exceed the locations capability in terms of runway dimensions. A compromise may suggest that an interim refueling stop may allow the use of a runway closer to the destination. (Keep vertical or short takeoff and landing capable aircraft in mind when determining the solution set to optimize time.)

3. Nominal time in between these two points – what is the time that your passengers would reasonably like to spend getting between the two points. That may seem like a facetious question, of course they would like to get there as fast as they can, but defining what reasonable is to your passengers or customers is key to answering this question. As an example, if you are based on the west coast and have frequent meetings on

the east coast – speed and covering the distance between these two points is essential. While there are many airplanes that will make this trip, only a select few will cover this distance flying at .92 Mach. If your passenger or customer wants to depart the west coast, have a lunch meeting on the east coast and be back to the west coast in time for a late dinner, then your you have defined a key parameter. Once you provide the short list of aircraft capable of completing that mission, the cost will not be average, and that point may help define "reasonable".

4. Number of People (Payload part A) – Another key part of this equation is how many people are the typical passenger payload for your mission. An airliner may have an unlimited amount of customers that are lining up for the trip. A private operator may only have one or two. Another subset of this equation is how much cabin space does your customer base require, i.e., full stand-up cabin, larger seats with a lot of leg room, how about the noise factor, stand up lavatory, seats that berth for sleeping, separate cabin zones for sitting, eating, conversing, pressure differentials, communications and entertainment.

5. Amount of Cargo (Payload part B) – Not only is the number of passengers important, but how much cargo or baggage will each typically carry? Will they need access to their baggage while in flight? Unusually large baggage or cargo may not fit through baggage doors, think skis, large golf clubs, bicycles, sports gear. Here's an unusual one, one mission called for accommodating a four wheeled vehicle in one design, even large animals.

6. How frequently will the aircraft be operating and what will the typical flying hour demand be in a given time period; normally a year is the budget timeframe. What is the nominal flight time compared to the cycle time. Are coast to coast missions normal, international missions; this will be important as you work out the details for the mission statement and determining the size of the team.

Mission example:

1. *Guest travel from China to the United States and back. The aircraft used were Gulfstream G-550s or Boeing Business Jets (BBJ-700 NG). The BBJ aircraft had 15 passenger seats, the other 19 seats. The BBJ had a stateroom and another bedroom area, lounge area, two lavatories, full galley, crew rest area for two crewmembers, on-board storage area, even room for a treadmill, it flew at a maximum altitude of 41,000 feet with a high cabin altitude and max speed was Mach .80 with typical cruise at .78. The Gulfstream G550 had; a crew rest area for a single crewmember, one and a half lavatories, four place club, two place club with a divan, four place conference table, full galley in-flight accessible storage area, it flew at a maximum altitude of 51,000, cruised at up to .885 Mach with typical cruise at .80 - .83.*

The Gulfstream was faster, had a lower cabin altitude in flight but the BBJ was more spacious and allowed for more movement and open area. But it all was based on passenger preference, just as many passengers enjoyed the BBJ on flights from Europe or Asia as did flights aboard the G550. Passenger preferences are the important perspective and should be heavily weighted when selecting options and courses of action when determining which aircraft is appropriate for the mission.

Chapter Seven - Aviation Finances

Aviation financials are a topic that we must discuss. Although it is a painful part of any Aviation leader's job, some organizations are easier than others. Aviation centric organizations normally have financial business partners that understand the details around Aviation but other organizations will require a lot of information – particularly companies or individuals that have never owned or operated aircraft before.

The Aviation leader needs to determine where the organization is on the aviation experience continuum and prepared appropriately. It is vital that the Aviation leader has both the knowledge and experience to provide the information in the financial managers language and adapt the information on the level that provides clear understanding.

Everything starts with the mission. Understanding what needs to be accomplished, the definition of success and having a clear direction from the organization's leadership team will help the Aviation leader to aim and hit the center of the expectations target.

The budget estimate is where the Aviation leader excels and pardon the expression, but "makes money." The Aviation leaders budgeting worksheet, or compendium, is the base line for budget development. It doesn't matter what format is used, what matters is that the Aviation leader accounts for all the details and accurately predicts financial resource needs. Just like any budget exercise, the accuracy is all in how you capture the costs and accurately list these details.

Here are some of the basic information details that you'll need:

1. Type of aircraft operated (may be multiple types, normally categorized as company owned or leased, charters, or contracted) which results in total aircraft available or budgeted for)
2. Number of flying hours anticipated in each type for the budget timeframe.
3. Account for owned (organic) and shared aircraft separately as the budget amounts are different.
4. Number of crew members for each aircraft. Stay focused on the mission during this calculation and be

considerate of crew duty time requirements, training, off-time, etc.

5. Number of maintenance technicians required for each aircraft – same as above, stay focused on the mission requirements as the number of team members are needed.
6. Staff number calculations includes Operations Team members, HR, Finance, Security, Aviation leaders, i.e., Safety Manager, Chief Pilots, Chief Flight Attendants, Operations Managers, Chief of Maintenance, Facility (FBO) manager, Travel manager, Administrative staff, Refuelers, Ground Support Teams, Temporary or Contract Staff Costs, Aviation Leader.
7. Calculate the total compensation costs in addition to direct salaries (Awards, Bonuses, Workers Compensation Insurance, Health Benefits, moving costs, payroll taxes, etc.)
8. Facility costs
   a. Lease costs, rental, amortization, taxes
   b. Facility maintenance costs – HVAC, lighting, fall protection.
   c. Facility equipment maintenance
      i. Forklifts, tugs, lifts, compressors, tools, hangar doors, air hoses, power cords,

ground power units, ground hydraulic power units, floor cleaners.
   d. Facility utilities – water, electricity, natural gas, sewage,
   e. Facility fuel oil facilities – storage tanks, supply trucks, pipelines
9. Facility and Operational Ground vehicle support
   a. Maintenance
   b. Leasing, Financing, Amortization
   c. Maintenance
   d. Inspections
   e. Amortization and Depreciation
   f. Taxes
   g. Permits and licensing
10. Aircraft costs, includes:
    a. financing costs,
    b. leasing costs,
    c. amortization and depreciation calculations,
    d. maintenance costs, includes scheduled maintenance costs, hourly reserve costs, and maintenance program costs,
    e. insurance costs
    f. databases and subscriptions, including computerized maintenance program access or software, operating information for flight

operations and navigation (Approach plates and enroute charts, weather services), OEM pilot and maintenance software accounts and access

    g. refurbishment reserves
    h. communications
    i. entertainment
    j. catering
    k. cleaning and servicing
    l. deicing
    m. property taxes
    n. business license costs (regional requirements)
    o. Remote operations (Away from home base facility fees, ramp and parking, security fees, hangar fees)

11. Fuel Costs for each type of aircraft
    a. Calculated by average cost per hour of fuel consumption
    b. Include taxi times, auxiliary power unit run times.

12. Travel costs
    a. Crew meals
    b. Hotels
    c. Rental cars, ground transportation
    d. Airline tickets

13. Training costs

a. Pilots
   b. Flight Attendants
   c. Maintenance technicians
   d. Operations
   e. Security
   f. Safety

14. Indirect Costs
    a. Office supplies – allocated by person
    b. Aircraft supplies – service items, linens, entertainment, customizations
    c. Operating supplies – cleaning items, oxygen, nitrogen, hangar maintenance costs
    d. Technology costs – per person computers, iPads, phones (mobile and office), connectivity and data usage
    e. Shipping costs – couriers, shippers postage
    f. Uniforms – personal clothing, safety clothing and personal protective equipment, specialty items

15. Airport Operations Support
    a. Contracted control tower operations and maintenance
        i. Communications and connectivity requirements
    b. Ground operations and line support

  c. Facilities
    i. Furnishing
    ii. Maintenance
    iii. Entertainment
    iv. Technology – monitors, telecommunications,
    v. VIP lounges
    vi. Restaurants and food service
  d. Fuel and refueling
  e. Runway, taxiway repairs
  f. Airport general maintenance – lighting, painting, signage,
  g. General staffing costs
  h. Ground support vehicles and maintenance, similar to facilities vehicle cost calculations listed above (airport maintenance vehicle requirements are vastly different from flight operations vehicle support, fuel trucks, maintenance trucks, snow removal equipment, aircraft movement tugs, fire and rescue, and general grounds maintenance vehicles may be part of the overall requirement depending on the scope of the departments mission.

  While these budget areas specifically identify the operational budget development, in some organizations a capital budget is also maintained. The capital budget may include the following items, depending on the definition that the organization uses for capital budget development. Some examples of the capital budget:

Facilities costs and additions

Aircraft acquisition

Computers, Technology upgrades, connectivity

Finance and Budgeting is a basic requirement for the Aviation leader. Depending on the complexity of the greater organization, the most effective way to manage budgets are:

1. Have section/department leaders participate or develop their section's budget.
2. Use a two-step approval process for any money spent, the reviewer should be the person that ordered the item or service and authorize the payment, or in a situation where a credit is posted, review that the credit is accurate. The approver should have the authority based on the amount to authorize the payment.
3. Delegation of Authority Tables should be established in the organization. The Delegation of Authority shows who in the organization has

spending level authority for different categories of spend. Limits and Typical categories may be:
  a. $250 M/Projects – Studies for purchases
  b. $5.0 MM/Contracts – consultants, services, purchases.
  c. Capital Budget - Projects
  d. Charitable Contributions
  e. $200 M/Compensation Decisions – Salaries, Bonus
  f. $5.0 MM/Leases and Purchases
  g. $1.0 MM/Emergency Response
  h. $100 M/Travel and Expenses

The Aviation leader should verify this budget level authority with the senior leaders or principals of the greater organization.

Since Aviation organizations are generally one of the higher cost organizations within a greater organization, the details of any transaction should be completely transparent within the senior leadership team or principal owner(s).

The caution here is that sharing the Aviation organization's budget within organizations tends to draw a lot of attention. This can create a lot of questions. Since the Aviation organization normally runs higher budgets by virtue of what it does, it may not be necessary to discuss the Aviation organization outside of a small group that manages the budget.

Normally transparency is the right answer within the organization but given the relative scale of Aviation expenses compared to the remainder of the greater organization, it generates a lot of internal discussion that isn't beneficial.

The Aviation organization budget should be restricted to the need to know in greater organizations that are non-Aviation organization. However, it is managed within the greater organization, it should be a deliberate decision within the greater organization so that information shared is understood and managed discretely.

Simple information regarding refueling costs normally identify where the aircraft was refueled and other potentially sensitive information. As decisions are made within the organization, be sure to make deliberate decisions about who and what information regarding the Aviation organization budget and financial transactions have the need to know and understand the sensitivity and the need for complete discretion with the information regarding the Aviation budget. It is sometimes difficult for an accountant that may be managing a general ledger to understand and comprehend aircraft catering costs or general repair costs and keeping that in context or not be tempted to make general comments to co-workers.

Without sounding too secretive or anti-transparent, be sure to understand the risks of being open and transparent with the Aviation organization budget outside the "need to know" level and make deliberate decisions on how and who participates in managing the budget. If it isn't a deliberate process, there should be no surprise when general employee conversations in the break room focus on how much is spent on items in the organization that not everyone can access.

Chapter Eight - Interface with the Senior Leaders and Higher Headquarters – You Are Always Educating.

The Aviation Leader is the center of communications and education for all things Aviation. If you are in an Aviation organization this becomes a little easier since you are presumably working with other Aviation professionals.

The hierarchy of the organization, the number of other people that are working to support Aviation operations may or not be sufficiently versed in Aviation to shorten conversations.

As an example, if you are working in an Aviation centric organization where Aviation is the business and the revenue generator, some common Aviation challenge and solution conversations may be easier since you won't have to start at the beginning. You may be able to jump into the conversation at a higher level and not necessarily have to start with the Wright Brothers first flight or Montpellier's ability to pioneer ballooning.

If you are supporting a business that doesn't generate revenue in the Aviation industry, be prepared however to go back as far as needed to provide information pertinent to solving the problems and more importantly – accomplishing your Aviation mission. Hopefully you don't have to start with "you breathe air and I breathe air", but there are rare examples where it may get just that basic.

We have all been in meetings where the Aviation centric problem is discussed and no matter what background or profession, everyone becomes an Aviation expert. Information gathered from cocktail parties, fiction-based movies, books, "I have a friend, son, brother, etc., that is a pilot perspective", and other points are normally tabled during the discussion. Especially when dealing with the top levels of leadership in the organization, it seems that everyone has input.

The key to these open discussions is to somehow make the point gently that we need to gather data and perspectives based on experience, not third-hand, internet-based, philosophical information. You have a unique responsibility. As the Aviation Leader, you are charged with the vital mission to fly aircraft, deliver people and goods from one location to another, safely, without harming, in any way, the people, the crew and cargo, in all types of weather, in a dynamic environment, spanning international borders, crossing vast an uninhabitable terrain at times, and doing it completely, totally and achieving the mission routinely at 100% always – you need the perspective of experience.

Hearsay, the internet, what others think, or feel is nice to know, but doesn't have any bearing on solving the challenges you'll face in Aviation.

Anyone in the group, whether in the Board Room or on the flightline in a leaders huddle just prior to engine start that says, "I've done this before and this is what was successful", gets the floor and their input is valuable. The point is, be prepared to educate and communicate constantly and be able to gently and in a non-ego bruising, tactful way that opinions and philosophies can be discussed later, but in a time sensitive environment we need vetted and proven solutions in order to solve the problem at hand.

There are always times where philosophy and ideas are needed to begin to identify the problem and develop solution sets and options. This type of discussion must happen between the Aviation and Senior Organization leadership team. Sometimes this discussion can take on an ambiguous form depending on the background of the senior leader. Every challenge or problem can be solved with experience, time, and money. If the senior leader understands the Aviation cost continuum – bigger, faster, farther is directly proportional to increase costs.

If money and time is truly no hurdle and the supported leader wants, what is wanted – your challenge is easy. Find an Airbus 380, Boeing 747-800, or a Gulfstream G-700 to do your mission, whatever it is. You'll have the biggest, the fastest and the farthest capability at the current state of the art. You are all set, in fact, you really don't need the information that I am covering in this book. But if you are in position to solve this problem, I offer my services to assist. Please email me at Stephen.Saflin@gmail.com! I have never been so fortunate as to be in an organization that has had that approach – money is no object – and would love to experience what that may be like.

Please don't take this the wrong way. There are organizations where they do know that Aviation is expensive and they want the capability that is the fastest, biggest, and farthest, but they understand that Aviation gives you one thing that no matter how much money you have, you aren't getting any more time. For this genius class of people, that have leveraged their intelligence into wealth, Aviation gives them a time multiplier – it is the ultimate "do more, go farther, in less time" option. They are truly the human cream of the crop – they are smart and, in most cases, they know what is important in life.

For those businesses that are using Aviation to generate revenue or support their operations, they are led by this same genius class of humans, and they realize that there is no substitute for fast travel than Aviation.

Speaking from my personal experience, I have seen leaders, Aviation professionals and non-Aviation professionals, that are way out in front of others when it comes to their capacity for intellect. They certainly get it. They understand that Aviation gives them an exponential advantage. They are driven by passion, and they want to solve problems to better humanity. They want to make the world a better place for everyone. They are truly members of the genius class. I have had the opportunity to be inspired by many of them and once you recognize that they are part of the genius class, support them no matter how difficult.

You're an Aviation professional and you can use your skills to support them to advance us all.

If you find yourself associated in an environment where one of these truly gifted people are the principal, you'll never find a more rewarding opportunity – I am not talking about physical rewards, but the overall feeling that you are part of something that contributes and has an objective that is much, much more than just a job – it is a lifestyle of service and if you are the right Aviation Personality Type, you'll never find a more rewarding feeling.

I'll keep this part as positive as I can… But, just as there are the genius class of humans, there are the folks that would like to be considered as part of this class – they self-identify, and it'll be apparent that they are not part of this class no matter how much they believe. The organizations that they lead are normally characterized by high attrition rates.

As an Aviation Leader, you'll be in a constant cycle of gathering information, anticipating, developing options to solve challenges, communicating information, educating, taking the planning, and strategizing and executing. It is an expanded deliberate decision-making process.

Deliberate Decision-Making Process

Identify the Problem – information gathering, facts and assumptions that come to bear on solving the problem.

Identify Possible Courses of Action – List as many possible courses of action, evaluate each based on the criteria that is developed from the objective (mission), facts (what you know), assumptions (what you think you know, but always categorize these assumptions during the sensitivity analysis of your courses of action)

Evaluate Course of Action – Experienced based factual analysis has the highest confidence interval for success.

Develop Plans to Implement the Course of Action – Communicate, communicate and the communicate the course of action in the simplest terms – misunderstanding a phase in the implementation has the same effect as selecting a sub-optimal course of action.

The plan should also develop contingencies and possible options for the selected course of action if the problem is dynamic. If you find a course of action is dependent on a variable, take the variable into account and develop an "if this happens, then we do this.'

Implement the Course of Action – act and make it happen.

Analyze during implementation and watch for the need to adjust at critical decision points.

Review Lessons Learned – Communicate with all stakeholders and those involved. Educate those that need to know the outcome.

Communications have never been easier. So, there is no reason for someone not to know something. Nor is there any reason for anyone to make the statement, I didn't know. If they didn't know, they didn't want to know. As mentioned before, communications have never been easier. Phones, text messages, live video communications, emails, there are so many ways to communicate. And sometimes that can be the problem. Communication inundation is more and more of a problem and since the communications are nearly instantaneous, there is more reaction to problem-solving than there is solid thinking before acting. Then there is the unofficial form of communication – an email passed from someone to another that may only be a fragment of the entire discussion. There is no reason to not know. And managing communications is critical to where we are in terms of our ability to communicate.

The chain of command should be a critical part of the official communications and messaging strategy. Every part of the team should know enough about the official communications channels so they can evaluate what is real and what is conjecture. Unofficial communications aren't credible, and they can bring about anxiety and unwarranted actions.

Communications strategies are important and there is a communications priority. Here are some ways to formalize the organizational communications strategies:

Priority

1. <u>Face to Face or Real Time Voice or Video</u> - Urgent, Time-Sensitive Communications – where immediate action and instructions or situation may be complex and need in-depth discussion.
2. <u>Time Sensitive Written communication (emails or letters)</u> – Time sensitive but a needed response can be with-in 24-hours or receipt of the original message or query. This should have a note that includes, Action needed. If it is time sensitive, include a note that states "information needed by" line in the heading.

3. <u>General Information that needs no reply but is providing information</u> (emails or letters) – Reporting on a situation, this includes information from a follow-up request or query – if time sensitive or acknowledgements are needed – state it, "acknowledge or acknowledge by" If the acknowledge by isn't completed, then revert to face-to-face or real-time voice or video.

4. <u>Unimportant information or "pings"</u> (texts, webpages, social media sites) – no due dates, no action required, not even important, really doesn't impact the mission if read, received, or acknowledged. Texts can be used for less urgent, need to talk coordination – someone may be in a meeting, driving, flying and can't receive or take an urgent voice message and a text may provide a notification – but keep in mind this may be helpful but not certain.

If is critical, use all forms of communication, multiple email addresses, business as well as personal media, phones emails in order to get someone's attention. Official communications should always be using official, secure, company sponsored information channels. Just remember security level requirements. If you send an email on systems not using secure or internally secured servers, the information that is sensitive may find its way outside of secure communications.

Setting Up Routine Communications with Senior Leaders

Developing objectives, identifying problems and challenges, understanding intent requires frequent discussions. Many failures can be traced to misunderstanding which is directly related to lack of clear concise communications. Preventative measures can include meetings and discussions that communicate the problem or situation at hand clearly and concisely. Every tasking from a senior leader needs to have these questions answered before a successful course of action can be implemented:

1. The objective must be clearly defined – what are the key measures that must be completed to define the action as successfully completing the objective.
2. The parameters must include performance indicators that are measurable and defined.
3. The objective must be achievable given the time available, resources, information, and capability of the team responsible for the mission.
4. The objective has to be a task or something that the team or person can reasonable accomplish – if it requires superhuman abilities or capabilities it is a set up for failure – assign tasks reasonably
5. The objective should include a complete by time and date – if this isn't included in the tasking a reply of

"I'm working on it" is a valid answer to why it isn't completed.

The Aviation leader should always leave tasking meetings or meeting where actions are assigned with the information above clearly understood.

The chain of command or supervisor chain in Aviation organizations that gain revenue from Aviation activities are normally centered around a strong Aviation support organization. A supervisory chain within an organization where Aviation takes on a support or enabling role is different and varied.

While these organizations will have different leadership structures, it is essential to keep the Aviation department as close as possible to the senior leader that will be supported and provide the majority of the taskings.

Since this leader understands the value of the Aviation organization, any step down in leadership dilutes the relationship, makes it more difficult to understand the leader's intent. In the end it makes the Aviation organization's work to provide a service that exceeds expectations more difficult.

Non-Aviation organization support levels work best when they report directly to the person that will provide most of the organizations taskings. There are several categories that can define the non-Aviation organization for leadership and supervisory authority:

- Key to the success of the organization – this non-Aviation organization uses aviation support at all levels and understands that the Aviation organization is not just a luxury for the top few leaders.
- Organization that supports an individual and supports the person who understands that they cannot accomplish their deep-seated, driven objectives (single genius tasked organization)
- Organization that supports a group of individuals that have used Aviation for their needs, and it is customary.

Initial meetings with senior leaders take time. We sometimes forget that we are human and relationships matter. Taking this time to understand one another builds a basis for trust. Understanding the intent, the overall direction, and objectives of what the senior leader's or principal's vision of the Aviation organization is important to understanding and defining what must be successfully achieved.

The initial meeting should focus not on details, but on the general direction. To develop the mission statement, complete with stated and implied tasks, a general direction must be developed and clearly understood. If the Aviation organization is supporting an Aviation revenue generating operation, the mission and objectives will be clearer than that which supports the non-Aviation organization. But one thing must be clear to both the Aviation leader, as well as the senior manager, and that is the parameters with which the Aviation leader will operate; tightly bounded or in an environment where the Aviation leader can utilize the complete spectrum of their experience and capability.

Those boundaries must be clearly defined in order prevent confusion, hesitation and lack of objective attainment.

The initial meeting between a senior leader or principal of the organization should clearly define what is the principal's vision of the organization – getting to "what, how, when" are really the questions that need to be answered. For the non-aviation organization, getting to the simplest form of the mission statement is generally the objective during an initial meeting with a new leader or leadership team.

This may take a little time since they may not have thought about it in depth, or it may be a short conversation if the organization has a history of what it has done in the past.

They key takeaway is that the Aviation leader must know and understand what is required to develop a logical plan to support the mission. It may take several meetings if it is a new organization and there may be an exchange of what is needed or wanted, then feedback of what is a practical and realistic strategy to achieve it, within in the time and budget desired.

The start point is the who, what, where, when, how and why. Take notes, ask clarifying questions, provide feedback based on your level of experience and comfort.

This should be a conversation and the outcome should be that both the supported organization and the Aviation organization that is providing the support knows, understands, and can articulate the objectives in plain language. Translating all the stated and implied objectives should be used to develop the strategy. The questions of who, what, how, when, and why are apparent, clearly understood and actionable.

Routine and frequent conversations are helpful to re-affirm, re-direct, update and adjust the mission. Since this process is resource intensive, the reality may be that the vision, the reality and more importantly, the budget are aligned to support mission accomplishment.

The experienced Aviation leader knows and understands the resource requirement. They should have an idea of the scale and scope of the mission to meet the needs, but that isn't always the case when the Aviation leader is new to the organization.

If that is the situation, then the discussion may be more one-sided, and the principal can describe the vision. The Aviation leader will have to take time to review the organization and realistically determine the Aviation organization's current status or situation and overlay the requirement with the capability.

Normally, when this is the case, one of three outcomes are possible;
1. The Aviation organization has the capability, and no gaps exist to accomplish the mission (rare situation),
2. The capability of the Aviation organization exceeds the requirement (more normal than not),
3. The capability of the Aviation organization does not support the requirement (more frequent) and the Aviation leader must build the strategy to close the gaps If in the organization that has all it needs or more to accomplish the missions, the Aviation leader continually looks for ways to expand the Aviation organizations role so that it can support more needs within the organization and increase the value of the Aviation organization to the supported organization. The Aviation leader is always seeking to identify sustainment opportunities or improvement strategies.

Mission requirements – it really all comes down to knowing and understanding that as clearly and as soon as possible. Conversations needed to understand the mission requirements fully vary and that is the dynamic part of this process. It may be a quick, or it may be an uphill battle, but before the Aviation leader does anything – the mission and the definition of success needs to be understood.

During the initial mission definition meeting(s), the path to knowing success is vital. How else will the Aviation leader know they are proceeding in the right direction. Interim measures of success may need definition if the mission is lengthy and complex.

The Aviation leader should use their experience and knowledge to understand how success is measured. That is the perfect world, but reality is that most non-Aviation principals may not know how to define that. As a word of caution, it takes a lot of patience and time when working with a principal that doesn't know what they want, but they'll know it when they see it. The "it' can be illusive, indescribable, and unattainable. They may not know the depth and complexities of the Aviation organization, but the good news here is that is why they have hired an experienced and competent Aviation leader – the importance of "getting along" cannot be overstated. The mesh of the intricacies of personalities and styles is critical, but overall, it is the Aviation leader's responsibility to adapt their style to the principal's style. I cannot stress this enough – the cultural fit within the organization, as well as the ability to adapt to the principal's leadership style is critical and the synergies are infinite if compatible, if not, every day will be an exercise in frustration. If the Aviation leader finds themselves in this situation, then it is incumbent upon them to step away from the organization. This guidance prevents frustration, misery, and eventual failure for the Aviation leader. This guidance is not just for the Aviation leader, it also applies to every member within the Aviation organization. It is incumbent on the members of the Aviation organization to make sure that they are compatible with the organization type, culture, and leadership styles. Mismatches and cultural inadaptability create intolerable stress within the Aviation organization.

Many Aviation leaders fall into the trap of comfort and compromise. They make conscious decisions every day in some situations to compromise when organization cultures and types are not compatible, but they force the fit for a myriad of reasons, based on their perceived level of comfort. Comfort with their lifestyle, salary, aircraft type, overall organization, and cultural environment.

Anyone can be who they are expected to be during one-hour interviews, but it is important to ask the key question – is the culture, the social environment, objectives, Aviation organizational type and reporting structure something that is compatible with the Aviation leader, as well as any Aviation team member.

You may fall into a trap of thinking that you are such a dynamic leader and can effect change but make sure that the gap that exists between your style and personality and the organization's or your principal's can realistically be closed. The capable and experienced Aviation leader must have a clear vision of success and just like anything we do in Aviation, the plan is deliberate, well defined, and apparent.

Spending the time up front to make sure that the vision, objectives, and performance expectations are clear, well-defined, and attainable is one of the most important, if not the most important factor that sets the foundation for everything and everyone within the Aviation organization.

Any competent Aviator wouldn't takeoff without knowing the destination and landing point, an Aviation Maintenance Technician wouldn't complete a maintenance action without research, an Aviation Operations Specialist, Scheduler or Dispatcher wouldn't task an aircrew or aircraft without knowing all of the details of the requirement... the Aviation leader needs to have the same discipline in getting the information needed to complete the mission statement for the organization and this comes directly from the principal or organizational senior leader that leads an Aviation organization.

If you are a principal, aircraft owner, or organizational leader that has the responsibility for the flight department or Aviation organization, please know that the Aviation leader you are working with is a near perfect blend of passion, enthusiasm, reality, capability and experience – with an infinite love for their craft – and an attitude and aptitude that makes them perfect for the task at hand.

They need four things to do the job that you want them to do:

>Information – who, what, where, when, why, how.

>Time – enough to analyze, plan, decide and execute.

>Resources – enough to accomplish the mission.

>Training – to adapt to specific requirements.

Aviation leaders all start out to do the job that you have asked them to do.

The one thing that they cannot continually do is justify why they are there.

Aviation organizations that the principals and senior leaders of the organization will make very deliberate decisions to have an Aviation capability, a capability that is reserved for those who understand that the Aviation organization gives you one thing that you'll never have enough of – time!

An aircraft is a time-machine and organizations know that is just as precious a resource as any other resource. The organizations that make the deliberate decision to add this incredible and unparalleled ability have a distinct advantage over others by having the flexibility that having access to an Aircraft offers.

Asking your Aviation team to justify that is easy, they know it better than anyone.

What is more important is that the supported organization knows it and supplies the four needed components to the Aviation organization – the time to do the mission, the resources to do the mission, the information to do the mission and the training to do the mission.

Those four components are essential and if not articulated in sufficient details or quantities – the chance for success decreases.

Aviation professionals are relatively superhuman when you think about all they can do, but they can't be required to perform superhuman feats every day to make up for the items mission in those four components.

Initial Leaders Discussion Outline

- Background discussion – developing the common frame of reference.
    - Senior leader experience in Aviation leadership
        - Aircraft already in place
        - How long, experience with regulations, performance, maintenance, SOPs, policies, SEC, GAP, IRS reporting requirements

- Hands-on or hand's off management style – how much information is too little or too much – Aviation leader leads off and adjusts as needed.
- Phone calls, emails, texts, face-to-face level of information sharing – what is their opinion of what is appropriate.
- How often, daily, weekly, monthly, call when needed?
- Reporting philosophy – Bad news doesn't get better with age, report anything that isn't going according to expectations, offer options for corrective action.

- Objectives Discussion
  - What is the vision for the Aviation organization?
    - Safety Philosophy – whatever it takes to maintain safety (is really the only acceptable philosophy)
    - People Leadership – staffing levels (reliance on superhuman effort all the time; or appropriately staffed to maintain consist of support levels)
    - Latitude of people decisions for the Aviation manager – responsible for building and maintaining the team – what about Aviation Personality Types (reward

those deserving, help for misalignment, does the Aviation leader have the lead on these decisions)
- Operations standards – cutting edge, leading edge, or trailing edge.
- Fleet planning – status quo, modernize, missionize, philosophy (cutting edge, leading edge, or trailing edge)
- Budget Management – centralized or autonomous, what latitude does the Aviation leader have when spending money, committing the organization for financial obligations (discuss Delegation of Authority limits).
- Definition of success, ask for examples of where other organization leaders have been successful.
- Initial plan and strategy – the recap of the discussion, what was heard, in own words, if this is done does that meet expectations…

Next Steps – Combine the Strategic Objectives of the Greater Organizations with the Aviation Department

This part of the process will take the discussion between the Aviation manager, the principal or senior leader of the organization and translate those thoughts, ideas, visions, and objectives into tasks for the organization.

The Aviation mission should be integral and directly correlated to greater organization strategic objectives and goals.

In its purest form, the words, thoughts, and vision are translated from the ambiguous into actionable information.

All that is needed is for someone in the organization to pick up the task and make it reality.

While the Aviation leader is responsible for all of it, including if it doesn't happen, the specific ownership of the action is needed to ensure success – group owned or diffused responsibility never worked and never will. Assign the objective, give them the information, resources, time, and training…

The organization may have lofty goals that are difficult to translate into the Aviation mission, but it is all possible.

The important part is that everyone understands what needs to be done, how to do it, and by when it needs to be completed.

For example, most organizations have "achieve excellence or sustain a high performing organization as one of its goals. Aviation training, attending seminars, leadership development training and similar programs all are directly related to the overarching organizational strategic objective to sustain a high performing organization. Many organizations will include financial objectives as well and if you are part of an Aviation organization that is a cost-center, rather than an Aviation-centric revenue generating organization, fiscal responsibility from the Aviation organization can support this objective. Money saved by the Aviation organization can be directed to the business units that are revenue rather than cost centers. An objective that seeks to develop money saving long term training contracts may be included in the Aviation organizations objectives and directly supports the financial objectives of the greater organization.

More simply stated, the Aviation leader should take the general organizational goals and translate them into actionable goals for the Aviation organization and cascade each into the individual's performance objectives.

Example:

Organization's overarching goal: Financial Objectives – Increase shareholder value and return value to the shareholder.

Aviation Organization goal: Minimize cost for away from home base fuel purchases and expenses.

Aviation Leader goal: Utilize contract fuel and develop relationships with frequent destination FBOs to leverage loyalty into fuel cost savings.

Aviation Operations Specialist's goal: Develop relationships with contract fuel providers and FBO to leverage loyalty into fuel cost savings.

Aviation Flight Section (Pilots): Tanker fuel when it makes sense to avoid high-cost fuel purchases, or when not an option work with Aviation Operations to use locations when able to minimize fuel costs.

Warning: Using fuel savings as an example does not mean that this supplants safety and any safety consideration – running out of fuel is a fatal mistake and should never be used as a leverage for saving fuel purchase costs. All things being equal, if you have an opportunity to negotiate lower fuel costs and taking the same amount of fuel required to complete the mission safely – this would be a strategy to help the organization reduce cost – but never reduce safety margins. Plan your flight, including fuel consumption and reserve calculations – and fly your plan! Any experienced pilot will tell you that there is nothing more stress-inducing that worrying about fuel. That is a prime example of a self-imposed stress.

Once the plan is in place – communicate it!

"Tell them, tell them again and then tell them once more."

Even with that philosophy, you may have to continue to have conversations around objectives. It is important that everyone understands what must be completed to achieve success. One thing about communications, you can never overcommunicate. That is usually when the plan starts to fall apart – insufficient communications.

How to get the word out

Developing a communications plan is just as important as developing a budget plan, more so if key financial objectives are cascaded to individual performance objectives.

Team updates using texts, emails, phone calls, web pages, newsletters, coaching conversations, and meetings keep everyone situationally aware of who, what, where, when and why. Meetings at individual levels should be conversational and as frequent as the dynamics of the situation or information requires. Especially if the situation and information changes.

For the leaders and team members, more meetings may not be the answer, the level of participation may determine how frequently the meetings should occur. Aviation team members (refer to the Aviation Personality Type review in Chapter Three) that are professional and engaged, that like what they do, generally find ways to ask questions, engage in coaching meetings and general meetings to get the information that they need. The Aviation leader still has the basic requirement to provide information, time, resources, and training. Aviation team members need to have the right attitude and aptitude. Seems like we have the plan for success once we have these components in place.

Coaching Meetings

Coaching meetings should be conversational. There should be a 50-50 exchange of talking and listening between the leader and the team member during one-on-one coaching. That is the time to talk about the details.

General discussions in coaching meetings usually start like this: *"How's it going? It's going well. OK, we'll thanks for your time and keep doing what you're doing."*

A casual observer would call that an unproductive coaching meeting. It was a little too general initially. A lot of time was spent developing the objectives, why not start the meeting using the objectives as the center piece!

Specific discussions in coaching meetings starting like this may use time more productively and get to a level of engagement quicker, we want to get to the 50-50 exchange of specific and actionable information: *"Let's start with a review of your objectives, how are the meetings and time spent with our most frequented FBOs going, is that yielding an opportunity for savings..."* The specific questions directed toward the objectives can get to the critical conversation faster. Then move into the more generic discussion once the team member has had a time to get to the critical points that they may need help with.

Department Meetings

Department meetings are very valuable. Within the Aviation organization, there are going to be meetings that are held within the specific departments; Operations, Flight, Maintenance, Support, Finance and Facilities – each needs to happen with the leaders of those organizations.

Same theme happens there, create an agenda, work off the critical topics and get the information that the team needs collectively and individually. Focus on critical tasks first, discuss objectives and specific agenda items. Important milestone events: audits, critical operations (maintenance events, personnel hiring, important meetings that are supported) are key agenda items during team meetings. Focus on safety, people actions, safety and security, operations, logistics and communications.

Aviation Leadership Team Meetings

Aviation Leadership Team meetings are vital and where leaders should bring their discussion topics and needs list to the forefront of the meeting so that detailed updates can happen, challenges addressed, resource needs identified, and priorities established. Aviation leadership team meetings should be routine. It is amazing on what gets discussed even though the agenda may seem minimal or specific. Some of the ancillary discussions can be even more productive than the key topic. But that is the idea, making communications happen and setting the stage for productive conversation. Meetings become a conduit for productive communications. The more the team knows about the who, what, where, when, why, and the intent, the chances of completing the Aviation mission increase dramatically.

Specific Mission Briefings

Use specific mission briefings anytime the mission involves a collective effort. Audits, mass movements when more than one aircraft is involved, or any mission that is critical to the performance tasks assigned to the organization warrants a specific briefing. For these specific briefings the best format for getting critical information out in minimal time is the Five-Paragraph Operations Order (OPORD). The OPORD summarizes the mission clearly, specifically, and succinctly. It provides all and ever important who, what, where when and why in an organized method. Aviation leaders can de-militarize it and use plain-speak that suits the organizations character. Depending on the organization, use vernacular and context that best suits the culture of the organization. The example below demonstrates how the format used can easily be applied to administrative actions as well as operational missions.

Components of the OPORD and example:

Situation – describes in as few words as possible what is happening, "Our department is scheduled for a Financial Audit in December.

Mission – The Aviation team will provide information to the Financial Auditors and fully cooperate with the auditors until the auditors are completed. A successful audit is defined as completed on time with zero outstanding deficiencies found with outstanding actions.

Execution –

Aviation Finance will be the primary organizer of the audit. Aviation Finance will:

1. Coordinate with the lead auditor to define the specific schedule and details of how the auditor will conduct the audit.
2. Be the primary point of contact for any information exchange between the lead auditors.
3. Develop and publish the audit schedule.

Aviation Operations –

1. Coordinate with Aviation Finance to determine key team members that need to be available during the audit and work around the operational schedule.

Aviation Facility Support –

1. Coordinate with Aviation Finance to arrange for office and meeting space

assigned to the auditors during the audit.

Logistics –

1. Normal support plan

Communications –

1. Aviation Finance publishes audit status reports daily to communicate audit findings, corrective actions, and details.
2. Aviation Leadership Team assigns specific action items to team members as soon as the deficiencies are identified.
3. Aviation Finance will keep a running list of audit findings, actions items, action item status and specific team member assigned.

The OPORD can be scaled easily to the size of the organization. Military Operations Orders are scalable from the Theater level where hundreds of thousands of warfighters are involved to the Squad level that effects five members of a fire team. Whatever form is used, it needs to have the components of who, what, where, when and why. There are hundreds of publications available that define the specifics and components of the Operations Order. Putting one together effectively is both an art and a science.

Quarterly Updates

As discussed in a previous chapter, these are critical routine information briefings that key on the timing of the release of specific information and data that is vital for the team to understand how the organization is performing and what actions may be needed to align with the greater organization.

The format and content should be tailored to the needs of the organization, but it should be consistent so that the Aviation team gets accustomed to the format, information, content organization and priorities. The Quarterly update's objective is to summarize the state of the Aviation organization and compare the thresholds and draw parallels of accomplishments to the annual objectives in general terms. The specificity is entirely appropriate to the priorities and the level of information needed to keep the organization informed. The larger the organization and the more time that passes between routine discussions, coaching meetings and team meetings will govern the content's depth and breadth.

Summary

AS stated previously, meetings are a conduit for communications. The Aviation team is comprised of people that are smart, industrious, situationally aware, forward-thinking, disciplined and self-starters.

Just as the appropriate level of resources, time and training are vital to successful mission accomplishment, so too is the proper information. The team must know the objectives, the conditions, and the standards and that is primarily accomplished through the flow on information. Given that the Aviation team has the resources, time, training, and information, they'll accomplish any mission and your conduit needed to pass along the information can be through formal and informal meetings, get-togethers, emails, briefings, and any form of correspondence.

Chapter Nine - The Aircraft Acquisition Decision and Process – A Deeper Dive into the Details Around Getting a Gravity Defying Time Machine

Any Aviation organization needs the right machine to accomplish the mission and it is just as important as having the right team members. The previous section discussed how to define the mission, and this is the section for determining the proper aircraft to use to accomplish the mission.

Since all aircraft are compromises of capability and complexity, defining the mission and its specifics will be the foundation for selecting the right aircraft.

Unless you are part of a company that builds the aircraft, the Original Equipment Manufacturer (OEM), you aren't going to have the insider information on the details. Build a broad, experienced, and capable team to help with the decision. The team will be scalable depending on where you are in the process.

After you have defined your mission, especially with the input and buy-in from the senior leaders or the organization's principal decision-maker, you'll build your team of decision stakeholders.

The Aviation Aircraft Selection Team is comprised of the following, but not necessarily all involved at the same time:

- The organization's principal leader
- The organizational senior leader responsible for the Aviation organization
- The Aviation Leader
- The Aviation Leadership Team
- Aviation experienced consultants
- Aviation attorneys (both in-house and external)
- Organization Finance, including Aviation finance.
- Organization Treasury, Tax and Audit
- Organization Risk Management (Insurance)
- Organization Procurement
- Manufactures representatives (marketing, sales, customer support, technical support, engineering, manufacturing
- FAA Counsel
- Lending institutions
- FAA program manager

Now that the mission is defined, the next stop is to organize a meeting with an Aviation consultant. The Aviation organization has a specific mission, and it normally isn't built around knowing all the latest and greatest that is available in terms of aircraft, systems, capabilities and reliabilities. But an experienced, successful, Aviation consultant lives in this world every day. They can cast a broader net, bring vital information to the discussion, and save on purchase and transaction costs throughout the process.

Finding a good Aviation consultant is difficult. If they are good salespeople, they have the advantage and are able to leverage the sales skill into making the Aviation leader think that they have the experience needed to assist in the process. There are thousands of salespeople that hang out their shingle and strike out to sell airplanes. They are great salespeople, and they are great because they can present a convincing argument that is sound and logical tailored to the personality that they are trying to convince. The key is finding one that has the broad knowledge in the industry with key contacts to get the best aircraft, within the specific timeline and the best price.

The important attributes of an experienced aircraft consultant are:

- Experience working for an OEM.
- The number of new and used aircraft that they sell every year.

- The people in their organization that they have that supports the consultant's organization.
- The processes that they have in place to define values, sales statistics, and aircraft types.

Experience Working with an Original Equipment (Aircraft) Manufacturer

Working inside the OEM organization provides the "graduate degree" of experience in the complex process of designing, developing, testing, maintaining, and bringing a specific aircraft type and model to the market. This opportunity and experience cannot be gained in any other manner.

A consultant that has worked for and sold an OEMs aircraft has been completely immersed into the entire process of developing, manufacturing, and delivering aircraft. The experienced Aviation consultant knows firsthand the good and the bad, the limitations, capabilities, design characteristics, certification limitations, and maintainability criteria for aircraft design.

A good Aviation consultant knows the process down to the minute detail of the life limits of the design, has seen the testing, evaluation, flight test and service tests for the design. While they may not have been integral to the process, they know, understand, and apply the design's compatibility to the organizational need more readily than a consultant that doesn't have that experience.

While Aviation consultants do not have a qualification program. A consultant that has worked in the OEM world has had the screening, training, and process organization knowledge and detailed opportunity to see what goes on inside the OEMs process. That gives the experienced Aviation consultant the opportunity to know and understand the critical parts of the mission/aircraft compatibility requirements intuitively compared to a consultant that may have had other industry sales experience.

This training, exposure to the process and hundreds of opportunities working with customers and sales teams breaks the process down to its requirements and needs. Whereas a consultant without it has some ground to make up to cover the complete immersion inside the aircraft development, mission and compatibility process.

Just like anything else, the more times a person experiences an event, process, procedure, system, or complex situation and completes a task successfully, they have the opportunity to experience that is gained at every iteration and every level of detail.

An Aviation consultant that sells more aircraft and has a client list that can substantiate completing the process successfully is by default, going to have more experience.

Ask the question and if possible, substantiate the claim with references. The more iterations, the more exposure to the industry, the more research, the more knowledge and better the ability to leverage that experience to solve the mission/compatibility problem. The experienced Aviation consultant will have more exposure to the latest information, including sale prices, manufacturing costs, discounts, and pricing strategies. The experienced Aviation consultant can leverage this knowledge into more advantageous price-based negotiations not by giving specifics and details about previous clients or customers but by knowing the range of contracts written and therefore being able to assess if the selling price is comparable and competitive.

By this standard, an experienced Aviation consultant should be able to save more on the purchase price than they add to the overall cost of the process simply by advising the client that there is more room to negotiate a more favorable price.

And it doesn't end there. Since the aircraft purchase process can take some time, and the economic environment is dynamic, a good and respectable Aviation consultant will stay with you from initial discussion through to delivery and in-service placement. If at any time during this process, the Aviation consultant determines that there is an opportunity to re-negotiate any or open aspects of the agreement, there can be additional value that can be discovered and leveraged into overall cost savings.

Aircraft consulting, just like the Aviation organization is a team-based endeavor. The more detailed and broad experience the specialist has, the higher the chances of success. The Aircraft consultant should have on their team the maintenance, operations, finance, legal, and liaison specialists. Attorneys that know the details of aircraft sales and ownership, former maintenance chiefs, pilots, and operations managers, that have real world experience that can work with the Aviation consultant lead to solve the specific requirement problems of the organization is imperative. Going back to the previous paragraph, experience is what gives the solutions to complex problems the highest chance of success. Learning as you go is certainly valuable, but if there is an opportunity to hire the most experience Aviation consultant available, it will vastly improve the results.

Data based decision-making is critical in many Aviation organization decisions. Information that has credible detail on aircraft values, trends, depreciations, options pricing, value, in-service time, operational and dispatch reliability, tax valuations, as well as the number of aircraft of that type in-service and on the market can provide valuable information when it comes down to selecting the right mission/compatibility solution.

The more the defined and detailed the levels of data that are available to address the evaluation criteria, the more accurate the solution. An Aviation consulting organization that has access to the data that is maintained through and by their research adds confidence and credibility. The more data maintained, the more likely it can be parsed and applied to providing the solution.

Summary

Find an Aviation consultant that has OEM sales experience, has been involved in the most sales transactions that have had successful outcomes, can leverage a team of internal experts, and maintains a database that can be leveraged to a successful solution.

The initial discussion with the Aviation consultant should start with the confidentiality agreement. Any information regarding details that can be associated with the intentions of sale or purchase process must be maintained in strictest confidence. A non-disclosure agreement that clearly spells out that everything discussed in Aviation organization to Aviation consultant meetings is restricted and not to be discussed with any other party without written permission that identifies what will be discussed and who is authorized to receive it. Any violation is a breach of trust and further work together should be immediately terminated.

The discussions after that are very specific and contain highly confidential information that can include, number of aircraft, type of aircraft, based locations, number of passengers, destinations, names of passengers – all of which is completely confidential. The rule of thumb is that the information discussed is not yours and not within your authorization to determine who can have it. Proprietary information and the ability to maintain it is the basis for trust. Trust must be valued by both parties.

Once the mission parameters are defined, collecting information about what is available now and in the future is part of developing the solution set to solve the problem of what is available and what can best support the requirements.

Now and in the future, availability has to be defined and while the current requirement may have a more time-bounded solution, there may be an option for an interim solution.

As an example, the mission requires an aircraft that is not currently certified, but the experience Aviation consultant knows of an aircraft that meets the mission requirements and is scheduled for certification in the future. The solution set for this example may be an interim aircraft. This is but one example of how important it is to understand the broad picture of what is available and possible. There may be a previously owned aircraft available to support the requirement while a new aircraft opportunity is contemplated. That solution provides a support option with an interim aircraft while the better support option is developed and delivered.

Once the strategy, type of aircraft and options requirement are determined, reviewing the options is the next step. This part can be time consuming and arduous as it may involve seeing the aircraft that are identified in the solution set, gathering detailed data pertaining to the specifications, descriptions, performance, and costs. Each aircraft identified must be reviewed and the capabilities compared to the selection criteria.

For example, the aircraft mission is typically a 4,400 nautical mile trans-Atlantic flight. Any aircraft that doesn't have the range would require a fuel stop, but any aircraft that exceeds the range of 4,400 nautical miles can achieve the requirement to fly between the two non-stop. So, any aircraft that has a practical range of 4,400 nautical miles or greater is acceptable. But an OEM submits a proposal that identifies that even though it doesn't have the range required, it does have sufficient speed that it can close the distance in less time at high-speed cruise with a fuel stop than a full 4,400 nautical mile aircraft can fly between the two points and lists several viable options to refuel – just an example of how important that developing the comparison criteria really is and conducting a practical sensitivity analysis of the criteria. Are there any criteria weighted more heavily than the others? The good news is that this is amendable and as you gather more information, you may adjust the criteria and what originally was not an option, may very well be highly successful.

The aircraft decision is a big decision and if the senior leaders or principals are selecting the best aircraft to the Aviation team, take the time needed to explore every option and identify the criteria. This may be a learning process for those not familiar with the type, size options and cost of aircraft. And, just as mentioned before, keep everyone in on the information and provide detailed updates. Ensure that all users and stakeholders can review the options and the interim decisions so that once the solution appears (the aircraft) on the flight line, the is no doubt, by anyone that what was selected, was the perfect choice.

The Critical Criteria

Here is a list of what is important, to name but a few:

- Getting from point A to point B reliably and safely – this is the primary criteria.
- Speed – what is acceptable, required and expected.
- Range – what is acceptable, required and expected.
- Service Ceiling – at what altitude or height above mean sea level can the aircraft operate.
- Cabin size – space inside the occupied area of the aircraft; length, width, and height

- Interior options – seating, berthing, or sleeping, food service preparation and storage, on-board amenities; showers, storage, baggage, amenities)
- Communications options – streaming, live, video, data rates, connectivity geographic limitations), including avionics – what communications, navigation and connectivity requirements are there for each region or area of operations.
- Reliability
- Maintenance program costs and frequency
- Cost – determine to life-cycle costs as well as the Net Present Value (NPV) calculation.
- Purchase strategy – purchase, lease, loan (each may define capital requirements, review the NPV analysis, internal cost of capital, any other sensitivities like balance sheet visibility)
- Ground support requirements – physical dimensions and weight
- Performance criteria – runway length, extended over water operations requirements.
- Cabin pressurization and noise levels
- Crew accommodations for length of duty day
- Crew requirements (pilots, maintenance technician, cabin attendant, others)

The following information may span a spectrum from simple to more complex. But since this is an important part of ensuring that the right aircraft for the mission is selected. A broader spectrum of knowledge was assumed to have the stakeholders on the same level of understanding.

Getting from Point A to Point B – Developing the list of aircraft that can accomplish the mission.

An aircraft is usually desired because it traverses the different types of terrain and geography faster than most any other type of conveyance. It is generally the fastest form of transportation and offers the most flexibility, so it rises to the top of anyone's wish list that wants to do more in less time.

Just like any other conveyance or form of transportation, its primary job is to transport people and things from point A to point B. Let's face it, if it can't do that reliably, it is a museum piece, hangar art or something that will still cost money and need maintenance. While the principal may like the acquisition cost of the 15-year-old aircraft, it is important to identify and articulate the shortcomings that may make this reliability unsustainable.

How far (distance or range) and how much (how many seats and how much cargo space) are the best place to start in developing the possible aircraft options list. Distance or range is normally listed as the distance in nautical miles that an aircraft can cover before it must be refueled. Payload is normally defined as number of seats available to be occupied for takeoff and landing -safety requirement - and how many pounds it can carry given the design of the aircraft. Once the distance and payload requirement are identified, the task becomes more simple to identify what aircraft types exist that can accomplish that mission.

The Aviation team and the Aviation consultant have a defined requirement that identifies the problem, and the next step is to develop the list of possible solutions given the typical distances and payloads.

Review all the aircraft that provide the desired capability to traverse the distance and carry the people, as well as the things that need transported. Depending on how specific the requirements are, influences what can complete the mission. Criteria in the left column and aircraft solutions (model) in the right column along with range and payload capacity. Range and payload capacities should exceed the identified and agreed upon requirements.

Now that the most basic requirement is defined, we can move on the additional criteria.

Speed

Your initial list of aircraft that meet the distance or range (in nautical miles, abbreviated NM, and payload (how many seats equates to how many people and how much cargo (cubic feet of baggage/cargo space and weight capacity in the cargo areas) can now be arranged by the cruise speed. How many nautical miles can the aircraft go in one hour in a no-wind condition – typically defines the cruising speed. Cruise speed is normally referred to as nautical miles per hour. If the aircraft has a range of 4,000 NM before it needs refueling and cruises at 400 NM/HR, then it can cover that distance in 10 hours in a no-wind situation.

Range

How far can the aircraft go without refueling. This range is normally standardized by convention and defined by the National Business Aircraft Association (NBAA) Instrument Flight Rules (IFR) Range designation. This puts a standard around the data by which the range is compared by using this summarized definition:

The distance in nautical miles that the aircraft can be operated without refueling by climbing at its best rate of climb to its service ceiling(s), cruise at the specified speed at the altitude(s), descend at flight idle at a specified descent speed, fly an instrument approach, and have sufficient reserves. While the NBAA range is a normalized range by which aircraft models can be compared, it is not a practical range for operational purposes. It is not practical since it is rare that an aircraft is given an unrestricted climb, cruise, and descent point. Weather, terrain, air traffic and other factors typically influence the operating parameters but rarely is it unrestricted. While range is defined by a linear measurement (nautical miles), there is another measurement – Endurance. Endurance is normally the time the aircraft can stay in the air at a given speed and it is normally measured in hours. It is critical to define the speeds when endurance is defined. Example, this aircraft has a 10-hour endurance at normal cruise speed. Endurance adds another facet to the aircraft capability definition.

Service Ceiling

The service ceiling of the aircraft starts to define the complexity of the aircraft. An unpressurized aircraft can normally operate at altitudes up to 14,000 feet mean sea level for limited periods of time. Anything above that without a restriction – meaning that it can cruise up to its maximum endurance limit at that altitude and it is normally conditional, i.e., long range cruise speed, normal cruise speed and high-speed cruise – requires a complex pressurization system, stronger cabin structure, and supplemental oxygen.

Cabin Size

Cabin size is the physical measurements of the cabin dimensions; length, width, and height of the area occupied by the crew, passengers, and baggage. As a rule of thumb, the longer the range capability and requirement, the larger the cabin requirement. The National Business Aircraft Association is one organization has standard definitions for aircraft that can be categorized according to cabin size. The definitions below may be helpful during discussions regarding cabin size (not a complete listing discussion but rather a generalization of cabin sizes):

Single Engine Propeller Aircraft – size range from automobile sedan to bus or truck sized aircraft cabin, generally no lavatory, ranges typically 600 – 1,000 NM.

Very Light Jet - size range from automobile sedan to bus or truck sized aircraft cabin, may or may not have a storage type container for a lavatory – defined as emergency use only, ranges typically 1,000 – 1,300 NM.

Light Jet – cabin width can accommodate single seat on each side of a narrow isle, no stand-up capability in the cabin for average passenger heights, longer cabins for more seats, limited layout, typically has a storage type container for a lavatory, may use curtains or solid walls for lavatory privacy, ranges typically 1,200 – 1,400 NM.

Mid-Sized Jet – a wider and longer cabin than the light jet and can typically seat eight passengers, not a true stand-up cabin, has a separate lavatory area that offers more privacy, ranges typically 1,400 – 2,400 NM.

Super Mid-Sized Jet – a wide and long body, seats eight to ten passenger, stand up cabin, may offer different seating options and zones. May have conference tables, and divans, limited galleys for in-flight service and a more private lavatory with internal baggage storage areas accessible in-flight, ranges typically 2,400 – 3,500 NM.

Large Cabin Jet – wide and long body, seats 12 passengers in wider seats, larger isles, flat floors, different seating zones, galleys, lavatories with running water and vacuum waste systems for waste, entertainment systems, in-flight accessible baggage storage, ranges 3,500 – 5,000 NM.

Ultra-Long-Range Jets – spacious cabins, stand up/walk around capability, lavatory, sleeping areas and furniture, long range flight crew accommodations, full-service galleys, refrigeration, ovens, microwaves, hot and cold water systems, vacuum waste water systems, multiple zone, divided cabins ranges typically 5,000 – 7,500+ NM.

Cabin size equates to comfort and is dependent on how many people and/or the distance travel requirement.

Interior Options

During the discussions and analysis completed by the aircraft acquisition team, the mission, range, speed, and cabin size were sorted out. Once these aspects are defined, the aircraft can begin to be defined from an options perspective. Cabin layout (LOPA or interior plan) is where the number of seats and type of seating takes shape. Smaller aircraft may have seats with folding tables, some that can recline fully to berth. Large cabins will have divans, credenzas, conference tables, galleys, crew rest areas, lavatories, storage areas, suites complete with bedrooms and private lavatories with showers.

The design and completion phase will take its requirements from the all-important mission requirements and work through the interior design process.

The interior design process is focused on the passengers. The senior leaders, the principal and even the principal's significant others can and should be involved in this process. Seats, materials, finishes, carpeting, refinements and interior appliances and equipment will be selected and designed into the completed interior. The larger the aircraft, the more decisions are made. Identifying key stakeholders, users and relating the design to the intent of the mission are essential to this part of the process. The finished product on delivery day should be astounding and amazing. It should be a functional work of art and a collective process where all the fabrics, finishes, appliances and equipment come together to create a breathtaking design that is overwhelmingly met with wonderful statements. Most of the OEMs and completion centers have designers, engineers and craftsman that can make the aircraft as personal as the owner or as functional as the organization requires. An aircraft is intrinsically beautiful and symmetrical, it is the perfect balance of art and science. Why not make the interior as appealing and fantastic as possible while meeting the requirements of what it must do – which is shelter the occupants from an environment so harsh that without it, they'd never survive.

Use whatever resources are available and affordable within the time constraints. Senior leaders, principals, Interior designers, automotive designers, yacht builders, maintenance chiefs, cabin crew, pilots, technicians, and any other stakeholder that has an interest should be able to provide input for the interior and options for the aircraft. Make it as personal as possible, provide updates to the design process with graphics, photos, and layout illustrations.

The Aviation organization's team and the passengers are going to spend time aboard the aircraft. It should be everything, everyone wanted. It'll be apparent on delivery day, why so much time was spent on the design.

The exterior of the aircraft is well defined by the design, but there is an option for personalization or customization – the exterior paint design. Small aircraft may allow a variety of colors, while larger aircraft may allow for base color selection, graphics, and paint layout. Here again, if the option to customize is available – take advantage of including as many stakeholders as possible and who has the final approval authority. When the aircraft appears on the ramp after delivery, the expressions should be a solid indication if the selection was successful.

For interior and exterior customizations, be sure to take full advantage of renderings, photo-realistic graphics, fabric sample boards, paint design layout graphics and models so be sure that all is captured and captured correctly. Most OEMs and completion centers that are experienced know that this is a vital part of the aircraft selection process, and they will have a myriad of tools and advanced technologies to have virtual walk-throughs, 360-degree imagery so that all stakeholders can see the results of the effort before it is applied to the aircraft.

Changes to the initial design are costly and influence the delivery timing. If changes are constant, it will slow down the process and delay the delivery. The Aviation leader has the unenviable job of relating the message that changes may equal increased cost and delivery delays.

Selecting Communications and Avionics Options

In the past. there was one point where aircraft had no communications options. Pilots used hand signals, towers used light guns and airport operators used flare guns to communicate with aircraft. Those were the early days of Aviation. Modern aircraft and aviation environments have access to nearly every form of advance radio communications as ground operators. Just about every way we communicate is in some form of visible or invisible energy wave form, is available in modern aircraft. Satellite communications (SATCOM), very high frequency VHF), wireless fidelity (Wi-Fi) and radio detection and ranging (RADAR) among other forms of wave energy are all used aboard modern aircraft. Options selection may include basic navigation radios, like an automatic direction finder (ADF) to live streaming audio and video from a satellite system. The process for communications option selection is the same as we discussed above; what does the mission require, what do key stakeholders want. For each new aircraft, there are options available – the Aviation leader should know what each is, what are the limitations, costs, and maintainability requirements (subscription costs) and ensure that the process is reviewed and has senior leader, principal, and stakeholder buy-in. There is nothing worse for the Aviation manager, on delivery day, for a senior leader, stakeholder, or principal to proclaim that they thought that they ordered the aircraft with an item, and it isn't there. Same process applies, communicate, communicate again and then communicate a little more so that everyone, has the same idea and expectation.

Reliability of the Aircraft Model

This paragraph is the subset of the initial paragraph, getting from point A to point B, reliably and safely. But it deserves a section all to its own. Reliability is safety, it is a component of value. An aircraft must be able to perform its intended mission 100% of the time when it is flying. It should have 100% reliability to support the schedule. If it is operationally ready, it should be able to start up, taxi, take off, climb, cruise, descend, land, and taxi to parking under its own power. If it can't do that then it has limited value. The statement of 100% of the takeoffs equals 100% of the safe landings may sound ridiculous but if the flight is only partially successful, it begs the question, what went wrong. And in the air, things going wrong doesn't equate to 100% mission accomplishment. For the Aviation leader to be successful, having mission reliability is an imperative.

Aviation leaders need to study the reliability of the aircraft in terms of overall reliability and dispatch reliability.

Overall reliability - measures how many days out of the flight year the aircraft is available to support the flight schedule.

Dispatch reliability - measures how many times the aircraft departed and completed its mission when scheduled. There is a third key metric, Mission Reliability.

Mission reliability - is the overall ability to conduct the mission, using a standby aircraft that is available if the primary aircraft is not available – in other words, aircraft number one was fully capable and scheduled for the mission, during pre-flight a discrepancy was found that could not be corrected before scheduled departure time. The back-up aircraft was moved into the primary aircraft schedule and assumed the mission. Take a point away for overall reliability, a point away for dispatch reliability for that specific aircraft, but if the mission is flown as scheduled and accomplished as expected – mission reliability remains intact.

The Aviation Maintenance Chief is responsible for aircraft maintenance, and therefore overall reliability and dispatch reliability. The Aviation Operations section takes the credit for overall mission reliability for having a backup aircraft available to assume the mission.

But any expectation must be aligned realistically with the fleet numbers. Older aircraft become maintenance dependent and need more maintenance as the fleet ages. Repair parts become less available and reliable, airframes begin to show age and need more frequent inspections and more frequent inspection and repair time means less overall reliability.

Aircraft model fleet dispatch reliability = 98% (means that 98 times out of 100 times, the aircraft was scheduled for its flight and completed its assigned flight as scheduled or expected)

Aircraft Overall Reliability is organization specific. Find the total days that the aircraft was available out of the year's flying hour program - 365 days, if the aircraft needed scheduled or unscheduled maintenance and was available for 200 days for an overall reliability rating of 54.7%.

The same aircraft had a 100% dispatch reliability which means that although it required maintenance 45.3% of the time, the Maintenance team did an amazing, heroic job of anticipating the schedule and have the maintenance completed so that it was available when scheduled.

For the above example, it suggests that the demand for the aircraft is low and the overall flying hour program for the aircraft is low as well. This may work well for the Keyed On Efficiency or Discretionary Aviation organization, where missions are scheduled at low-utilization number of hours, in the range of 150-hours or less per year. But for any other Aviation organization, the aircraft need to support the schedule when needed by the mission requirements for the organization, not fly when it is available to be flown.

Overall mission reliability tracks how often the Aviation organization met the requirements and was available to fly when needed. It normally is a factor and a metric when the Aviation organization has access to sufficient aircraft to schedule backups when required and the overall or dispatch reliability numbers are low.

The bottom-line here is that the Aviation leader needs to understand the aircraft reliability metrics, create realistic expectations for the overall organization based on those metrics and be able to communicate with senior leaders and principals the realistic expectations based on the overall fleet metrics especially when making aircraft acquisition decisions. If you are selecting a model that has a low overall reliability rating based on the age of the aircraft, or if the aircraft dispatch rating is low – a countermeasure may be required so that when the aircraft needs to fly, or a mission must go, an aircraft is available. If you are making acquisition decisions, select an aircraft that has reliability metrics that align with the organization's mission requirements.

Maintenance Program Costs and Schedules

As a continuation of the aircraft reliability section, maintenance program costs and schedules are part of the reliability metric. If dispatch reliability standards are maintained to meet the mission needs, how much maintenance time and parts are required to maintain those standards. The overall and dispatch reliability standard comes at a cost, and it is imperative that the Aviation leader knows the cost of maintenance.

Maintenance technician costs and headcount can be measured in terms of what is expected in maintenance time by the fleet for every hour flown. Is the ratio 1 hour of flight time equates to 1 hour of maintenance contact time or is it greater. Whatever the numbers, the metric should be tracked. What is the life expectancy for wearable items like brakes and tire? Is the aircraft or fleet meeting the expectations? The same metric applies for repair parts, how often are parts changed on the organization's fleet compared to the OEMs metrics. Maintenance cost expectations and the input from other operators or information collected by the experienced Aviation consultant can get this information for aircraft acquisition comparisons, and the Aviation organization can track that information on its existing fleet to determine if is the economical to operate and repair compared to other options. Most of the OEM publish maintenance time and cost requirements for their fleets but it is difficult to acquire, normally the Aviation consultant has some insight and can provide substantial information for time and costs. The Aviation Maintenance Chief tracks this information so that it is available for quarterly updates.

Overall Cost

Defining parameters eventually leads to a value equation decision – how much is available to spend or how much wanted to spend.

The option can be developed by one or two ways; What is the need or want and develop the cost model Or What is the available budget.

If the organization is either one of two types; Aviation Keyed On Efficiency Focused or Aviation Discretionary Focused, determining the aircraft options based on the organization's available budget to dedicate to Aviation operations it the best place to start. <u>Time can better be utilized defining what fits into the available budget rather than actual mission requirements if the organization cannot dedicate a budget required but rather what it can afford.</u>

If the organization is an Aviation Financial, Access or Mission Focused type, having the right aircraft to accomplish the mission is the important piece of the operating environment. It is normally a more mature Aviation operating organization that understand the flexibility and capability of the aircraft and the multiplier it brings to the organization or business. The organization has a sustainable model for use and has gone through several iterations of aircraft operations and has a clear and decidedly defined need for aircraft operations. <u>These types of organizations have a validated need, and the cost efficiencies are normally gained by comparing the aircraft needed for the mission rather than the aircraft that fits the budget.</u>

Aviation organization types aren't quantifiable in terms of which is best to operate aircraft but there is a clear difference in operational maturity and aviation operations savvy in the different types.

Non-aviation organizations that have not operated aircraft before and have not drawn sophisticated value driven equations for their businesses or organizations must experience the complexities, benefits, and differentiators that aircraft operations permit in order to have the ability and philosophy that drives to the right aircraft for the mission rather than is the available budget to support aircraft operations.

Trying to define the different Aviation Organizations is a difficult task without drawing a parallel to operations experience. Suffice it to say that organizations that are purely budget focused view Aviation operations as discretionary, if the organization or principal can afford it and it has an equivalent perceived value, then operating the aircraft is feasible. This may be transitory based on the financial ability of the organization or principal.

Tell-Tale Signs that Aircraft Operations or An Aviation Organization are Discretionary or Keyed On Efficiency Types
- Discussions on resources and training center on budget and perceived value and not the requirement to support operational best practices or regulatory standards.

- Aircraft are not utilized since perceived operations costs exceeds perceived value.
- Maintenance actions are delayed or heavily scrutinized because of cost.
- Personnel staffing limits operational availability or aircraft utilization is limited by personnel staffing.

During the cost analysis of the aircraft models that support the mission, it is not always possible to predict future costs accurately. The variety of factors that may influence the cost over the life cycle of the aircraft ownership should be compared. Training, maintenance, operations... as many components that impact the Aviation budget will have a range depending on the economic cycle of the economic environment both locally and globally. Since the Aviation leader needs to identify as many variables as possible that impact life cycle costs, it is important that the variables are included in the aircraft models under consideration. The only metric for financial comparison is the Net Present Value (NPV) calculation. It is difficult to forecast the movement of these variables. The comparison can be somewhat normalized by completing the analysis in Net Present Value. So regardless of the movement up or down for the variables considered, Net Present Value is the method to complete the comparison.

Please note – cost and budget capabilities are critical to manage in any organization so this section is not intended to state that an undisciplined or un-managed approach to an aircraft purchase is acceptable. For any level of success, a defined and realistic, attainable budget is highly recommended.

There are two primary methods to determine the required budget; either the budget is defined before the search for an acceptable aircraft begins, or the mission defined aircraft is selected, and the budget developed based on what is the right aircraft for the stated mission and the organizational/principal's requirements.

For new organizations, this may be the most critical part of the realistic and sustainable part of the budget planning. Experience has shown that this is the two most successful entry points on the basis for determining the Aviation organization's sustainable budget.

If it is a new, never-had access to an aircraft organization, determining the realistic and sustainable costs and associated budget requirements sets the foundation for the Aviation organization. Emphasis must be placed on developing a realistic and sustainable budget.

The organizational leadership or principal must be fully committed to the use of aircraft in the objectives and fully understand the costs and budget requirement.

Aviation has many very firm, solid requirements. Physical laws and regulations require adherence as does the minimum budget amounts.

If an organization displays any of the characteristics of a Discretionary or Keyed-On Efficiencies type organization, regardless of the Aviation leaderships team capabilities, the chance of sustained success is limited since the budget requirement is just as unforgiving as the physical laws and regulations. It is incumbent on the professional Aviation leader to ensure that the key decision-makers understand the requirement.

There are a variety of aircraft acquisition strategies available to the Aviation organization. There are a number of factors that may influence the financial structure, and each varies depending on the Aviation organization type. Specific strategies will be suggested at the end of this section once the different strategies are discussed. Regardless of the strategy employed, Aviation consultants, attorneys, FAA counsel and tax attorneys should be consulted.

Most organizations develop LLCs and Trusts as the structure for the aircraft ownership. A non-public entity at a minimum should create and maintain an LLC for the aircraft acquisition.

The LLC facilitates ownership by limiting liability, allowing limited anonymity, and facilitating the disposition of the aircraft.

Publicly traded organizations should consider creating a separate LLC, and Trust entity to limit liability, allow for limited anonymity and solve the ownership dilemma. For US Aviation organizations, aircraft registration requires that the entity is US owned and if a publicly traded company it may be difficult to guarantee that company ownership is maintained throughout the aircraft life span to meet the ownership requirements.

The experienced Aviation consultant and Aviation attorney is the primary advisor for the ownership structure, but the Aviation leader must be the decision-maker on the recommendation to senior leadership and principals.

Although this adds cost to the acquisition strategy, it follows the Aviation organization's intent to make deliberate action-oriented decisions and to do it right from the ground up.
There are different types of aircraft acquisitions.

Outright purchase – The acquisition can be an outright purchase from the seller to the purchaser. This is a cash transaction and normally has minimal interaction outside of the FAA Counsel/escrow agent, who normally places the funds in an escrow account until the final meeting where title is transferred, FAA and International registration is completed.

Financed acquisition – Involves the buyer, seller, and Escrow agent. Normally the purchaser will select the financial organization but there are examples where if the purchase involves the aircraft manufacturer, the manufacturer may facilitate the financing and may have lending institutions selected as business partners. Savvy, experienced Aviation organizations with substantial credit ratings are always favored by a broader number of financial organizations and may have credit facilities and relationships established to finance an aircraft acquisition. Experienced Aviation consultants that are involved in the sale may also assist in the financing options.

Organizations that are Key-On Efficiency and Discretionary may see fewer financial organizations offering to support the acquisition or the terms may be less optimal.

Before 2020, LIBOR, which was the London Interbank Offered Rate was the standard by which borrowing was graded. This standard will be phased out and replaced by SOFR (Secured Overnight Financing Rate). Pre 2023, LIBOR was the basis for aircraft financing, but since then SOFR or AMERIBOR (American Interbank Offered Rate), which established this benchmark but offers the same process of using a benchmark rate for banks on the American Financial Exchange.

Determining your financing rate is important as in any other financial transaction. Finance rates example:

Loan Amount: $20,000,000.00
$20,000,000.00

Term:	84 months	84 months
Interest Rate:	2.45% (compounded monthly)	2.45%
Monthly:	$259,337.57	$258,892.00
84 mos. Tot:	$21,784,356.23 $21,746,964.32	
Interest:	$1,784,356.23	$1,746,964.32

Takeaway: .05% rate difference adds ~ $37,392.00 to the cost of the aircraft. A two-point difference can add an additional $150,000.00. This should come as no surprise but obviously the goal is to be as value drive as possible and with large loan amounts be particularly sensitive to the interest rates.

Leased acquisition: A leased purchase is effectively just another method of financing the aircraft. This can have major financial impacts, so this is a great place to get the information needed from an experienced Aviation consultant, the organizations treasurer or financial manager, especially when large amounts are considered. An experienced Aviation consultant has the capability to compare financing options so that the Aviation leader understands the best options. To oversimplify complex analysis, there are essentially two types of leases:

- A finance (capital) lease as defined by ASC 840, is a lease where the lessee has obtained the funds from the lessor and can treat the asset as an owned asset (depreciation and tax consideration just as any other owned asset) and can be determined by answering four questions:

    Does the title/ownership transfer to the lessee at the end of the lease term?

    Is there a bargain purchase option?

    Is the lease term 75% or more of the remaining economic life of the asset?

    Does the present value of the sum of the lease payments exceed 90% or more of the fair value of the underlying asset?

- An operating lease as defined by ASC 842, is a lease where you pay the monthly lease costs and use the equipment, when you are finished with it, you return the asset (in accordance with the lease agreement). The lessee enjoys no benefits of ownership except to use the aircraft within the terms of the operating lease agreement.

When comparing the financial structure of the acquisition, calculations should use the Net Present Value (NPV) calculation so that all factors can be analyzed, and the true cost be compared. NPV is simply a method where all the calculations are done in the present-day valuations. If warranted. add a sensitivity analysis to the calculation to test how your decision is influenced by rate or term changes.

Leasing or financing an aircraft has certain benefits to the stability of the Aviation organization and the greater organization if applicable.

Leasing an asset normally keeps it from appearing on financial reports and allows a little less transparency except for the schedule that accounts for long term lease obligations. Most other benefits are applicable depending on the type of leasing, but other forms of acquisition normally allow for tax credits for expenses and depreciation.

The largest advantage from the Aviation organizations perspective is that a leased or financed aircraft is a little more difficult to turn into cash if an organization or entity needs to show revenue to keep the numbers up! A leased aircraft normally has language in the terms of the agreement that specify what must happen for early terminations. Costs can add up and a lease termination more than likely turns into a cost event rather than a revenue opportunity and that can take the "let's sell an aircraft to generate revenue to make the quarter" off the table.

As mentioned earlier, make sure that the team that is making decisions on aircraft acquisition is fully briefed and understands the costs and benefits associated with the deliberate decision to acquire any new aircraft. This is a recurring theme, so it has be mentioned before, communications are key and the exchange or critical information is a necessity in any Aviation organization. Aircraft purchases should involve as many key stakeholders as possible so that all the details are understood, the information is passed along, and any decisions have complete buy-in from the stakeholders.

Chapter Ten - Aviation Operations

The Aviation Operations team is at the center of everything occurring in the Aviation organization. They are the first responders of the Aviation team. For the Aviation team to meet its objectives, the Aviation Operations Team must lead the effort in anticipating, planning, and delivering the plan cleanly so that the maintenance and flight teams can execute the mission.

There are a lot of moving parts that are required to support the Aviation Operations Teams throughout the conduct of the mission.

Aviation Operations Team acts as the coordinating point for the mission support requests from all of the requestors, they must interface with Aviation Maintenance for available aircraft and the Chief Pilot for crewing availability. They must know the capabilities and performance of the aircraft and be able to provide information to the requestor on whether the mission can be supported. They maintain the records, for anything that is flight related and anytime an aircraft moves, they coordinate arrivals with FBO and organizations away from home base, work with third party providers and refuelers. They coordinate with government agencies for appropriate flight documentation, schedule hotels, airlines, rental cars, refueling, overflight permits, flight planning software, maintain policies and assist with any action that is required when an aircraft fly's.

For the Aviation Operations Team to function, they have the same requirements, resources, time, information, and training. The detailed planning that the Aviation Operations Team is capable of depends on the detailed and timely information that it receives.

Here's how it goes when it is going well.

Aircraft Authorizer - The Aviation Operations Team receives a support request from an authorize requestor. The first things that the Team must do is verify that the request is from an aircraft authorizer. The <u>Aircraft Authorization Listing</u> (AAL) is a by name matrix of who within the Aviation organization, and the greater supported organization who is permitted to use or assign for use one of the organization's aircraft. The authorization listing defines the priorities of support. For example, the Executive Chairman of the Board of Directors and the Chief Executive Officer are listed on the aircraft authorization matrix as the level 1 and 2 aircraft authorizers and receive priority of support in that order. The next level down in the organization is a level 3 authorizer and subsequent listings are defined until whomever the organization determines is an aircraft authorizer is exhausted. The Aircraft Authorization Matrix is essential so that everyone within the organization knows the order of the priority of support.

Scheduling – Once the Aviation Operations Team verifies that the request is from an authorizer, the team begins building the mission with all the requirements planned.

Normally the team would have a scheduling system so that the information regarding the schedule is available to the Aviation Organization and key stakeholders. There are many Aviation scheduling software programs available and depending on the numbers or aircraft, requestors and complexities, the aviation scheduling process should be maintained in sufficient detail for accurate records to be maintained. There are many different types of programs and scheduling software available and for as capable and affordable as these programs are, use them. They not only help with the mission planning, but they also maintain the records for the organization and document what actually has happened. Consult the Information Technology team or Business Partner to make sure that there are redundant pathways to back up the data and maintain it indefinitely. The flight scheduling information will be used many ways, for example, it will be used for compensation planning, tax planning, budgeting, usage information, and a myriad of other ways to reference trip information. Keep it as long as possible. If your organization has a document retention policy, make sure that your Aviation flight schedule data and aircraft usage information is exempt from any time limits so that it is stored indefinitely.

One last point regarding the scheduling software, a lot of information is going to be maintained with this software. All types of sensitive as well as personal information that must be safeguarded. The Aviation leader is not only charged with maintaining the safety of all aircraft operations, but also responsible for safeguarding the data that is collected and used in the scheduling process. Make sure that the software meets your scheduling software requirements.

Communicating the Schedule – The Aviation mission is the reason the Aviation organization exists. Scheduling information should be widely disseminated and frequently update, and updated in real time as soon as the change happens. There are many and varied opportunities to use technology to place video monitors in each office, common area, maintenance areas and ready rooms so that the Aviation schedule is posted and everyone knows what is happening. Use the system as a visual management tool – a large monitor that display aircraft status, taskings, team member schedules and aircraft flight schedules is the state of the art. Web or Cloud based access to the scheduling software should be available so that anyone with approved access can go to the schedule and determine what is scheduled in real time.

Aviation Operations Center – the ideal Aviation Operations Center provides all the tools and resources needed by the Aviation Operations Specialists. In a perfect world, it should have the ability to monitor schedules, airspace information, airport status, weather information, crew scheduling information, support staff scheduling information, aircraft live tracking information and any other vital piece of information that needs to be monitored and tracked so that the mission is successful. It should also provide an open area where face to face information exchanges can take place immediately if needed but also provide enough quiet confidentiality that is required to complete reports, make audio and video calls, support around the clock operations if needed and be comfortable and convenient so that it supports long hours of working through thousands of details each and every day.

The Mission Package – contains the information needed by the flight crews, those that are responsible to take all the requirements and the planning and make it all happen safely, securely and efficiently. The objective is to get the aircraft, crew, passengers, and baggage from the departure point to the arrival point safely and securely, and then be prepared to do it again to another destination. The mission package contents depend on the organization, but as a minimum it should contain the schedule, the details of the passengers itinerary, airport information, ground transportation, refueling locations, hangar or parking space, airport support capabilities, hotels, aircraft catering, and any and every thing that is needed so that the flight crews can do the mission. International travel adds additional complexities, Customs, immigration, agriculture clearance at arrival.

The Flight Record – is a concise log for updating and closing out the mission. The flight record for each mission could be as many segments as needed for mission completion. Departing from Pittsburgh, arriving in Miami, departing Miami, arriving Dallas, departing Dallas, arriving Pittsburgh contains three segments and each are identified on the mission log. The mission log that the flight crew receives for each mission should specify mandatory timing where the schedule is crucial to maintain, the plan may specify to depart 1030 local, but the flight did not depart until 1045 local due to weather and traffic. On the flight record the planned or scheduled timing is listed and the actual details are recorded for entry into the database to complete the record for the flight. As many details as possible should be included. Information to be included; tail number, aircraft type, mileage, estimated flight timing, flight crew, passengers, departure and arrival locations, specific location on the airport, radio frequencies, and most importantly, departure time as well as arrival time estimated and actual details. The Aviation Operations Specialist would then enter the details into the closed-out flight log.

Chapter 11 - Aviation Maintenance

If you have been in Aviation for more than a day, you have developed a very deep appreciation for a well-maintained, reliable, and always mission-ready aircraft. Completing the Aviation mission safely is an absolute requirement, and a well-maintained aircraft is essential to that mission. There are no shortcuts to effective maintenance, it is either maintained or it isn't.

Reliability was discussed earlier when discussing selecting an aircraft was the topic. In this section, Maintenance and reliability are discussed as an essential part of the Aviation Organization. There are many examples of effective maintenance programs, but all have one thing in common – the experienced Maintenance Technician. The experienced Maintenance Technician is essential to an organization that has an Aviation mission that relies on its aircraft to accomplish the mission. Aviation maintenance is accomplished in many creative ways, but organizational full time, contractor, or aircraft service centers are the only true ways for every aviation organization to keep aircraft fully maintained and ready to fly.

From the idea phase, through design, development, testing and entry into service, an aircraft and its components are made with reliability and maintenance in mind. An engineer stated during a design meeting that an aircraft is a host for parts. The airframe, which is the basic structure of the aircraft, or the shell, is assembled by metal stringers, ribs, stiffeners, and panels that create the wings, fuselage, empennage and tail assembly. It provides the housing and frame for the engines, environmental systems, avionics, auxiliary power systems, oxygen systems, batteries, lights, hydraulics, seats, carpeting, galley items, lavatory components, and the miles of wiring, electronic components, tubing, actuators, struts, wheels, brakes, and everything that it takes to make it a safe, maintainable and reliable air machine. Incredibly complex, yet simple at the same time.

The reliability is designed from inception to completion. Each component is tested to failure and the aircraft's initial certification specifies when, at a specific calendar time, takeoff/landing cycle, airframe, or engine hour level that it must be inspected, maintained, or changed. The components on the aircraft and the airframe itself, has a schedule for maintenance. It is detailed and specific. More advanced aircraft have sensors that monitor components and replay any critical conditions or limit exceedances to the maintenance, flight, and operations team. The safety and reliability built into a modern aircraft is remarkable.

But no matter how remarkable, it is a mechanical device, and it needs continuous maintenance from the first hour it fly's until it is retired and salvaged for the value in its metal.

Every aircraft has a life limit, some more than others. As an aircraft ages, inspections become more frequent, components and parts are more difficult to get, and reliability suffers.

With all of that said, with all the deliberateness in the development and design – an aircraft will always need maintenance. Depending on the reliability needs of the operator or organization, the amount of maintenance time differs based on the amount of flight time, lack of flight time or takeoff and landing cycles.

As mentioned previously, there are three key reliability metrics that the Aviation leader and leadership team must keep in mind and track.

1. Overall Reliability (OR) – this reliability index is normally tracked by the OEM or an organization that looks at cost data, reliability information and

supportability. Based on the number of aircraft in active service, an overall reliability factor may be the average based on the reported operations of a particular model of aircraft. The overall reliability based on a defined timeframe (calendar or flight hour) that the aircraft has for required inspections and maintenance. An organization with an aging fleet, may look at the regulatory organization for the service life extension program maintenance schedule. But in the simplest terms it is the days or hours that it is available for operations out of the total days in the period. An example, an airframe that has 20,000 hours or more may be involved in a service life extension program and out of a 12-calendar month time period, the aircraft must undergo a complete "teardown" type inspection where it cannot fly. Based on the typical maintenance shop capability, that may take six to ten weeks to complete. So not counting unscheduled maintenance the overall reliability may be 42 out of 52 weeks, or an 80% overall reliability. A newer aircraft with a progressive maintenance schedule may be able to use normal downtime for maintenance inspections so the overall reliability rate would be closer to 100%. An organization can track the historical overall reliability rate or the operational reliability rate by counting the days the aircraft is available to support the flight schedule over the number of days in the reporting period. OR = days available/days in reporting period. Any down time during troubleshooting, waiting on parts or undergoing maintenance and inspections would be a not available day.

2. Dispatch Reliability – this reliability index measures the time that the aircraft was scheduled for a flight and made the flight as scheduled. Any minor maintenance, fluid levels, tire changes, component changes with repair parts on hand that can be completed before the aircraft was scheduled and doesn't disrupt the schedule as planned, would not affect the dispatch reliability. But, as a convention, anytime the maintenance activity interrupts the mission as scheduled in advance of the flight, that goes against the Dispatch Reliability. As an example, an aircraft is scheduled for 100 flights, and it supports all 100 flights as scheduled without any maintenance impacts, then the Dispatch Reliability is 100%. If an aircraft misses the takeoff time or delay the takeoff time even if only one flight, the Dispatch Reliability is 99%. If the aircraft has three days where troubleshooting, maintenance or parts availability had prevented the aircraft from flying, and one additional

day where the flight was delayed beyond the scheduled takeoff time, then the dispatch reliability for that aircraft is 96%. Aviation organizations should compare the Dispatch Reliability of their individual aircraft with their fleet and the entire fleet of aircraft for meaningful data to be available. For example, one aircraft in the organization has a Dispatch Reliability of 96%, the organization's fleet of the same model aircraft has a Dispatch Reliability of 97% and the overall fleet per the OEMs number has a Dispatch Reliability of 96%. That important data set says a lot (other than the Maintenance Chief is a miracle worker). It substantiates that the organizational maintenance is highly effective and that the weakest aircraft's Dispatch Rate is equal to the overall fleet, but the organization's fleet is exceeding the overall fleet Dispatch rate. To put that into practical terms, out of 100 flights 4 will have to cancel for maintenance action at a 96% Dispatch Rate.

3. Mission Reliability – In fleets where there are multiple aircraft, an Operational Reliability Rate or Dispatch Reliability Rate can be less than optimal when other aircraft in the organization's fleet are available as a standby or spare aircraft. If the fleet consists of four aging aircraft, and only one or two is required for

mission support daily. The OR or DR may be 80% but the Mission Reliability Rate is 100% since the Maintenance Chief knows that a standby aircraft must be available since the aircraft reliability is reduced, but regardless of the maintenance status, a standby aircraft is available so that the mission can be supported.

To maintain aircraft, an organization has to have experienced maintenance technicians, tool sets, diagnostic and special tools, a maintenance facility with electrical power, lifts, compressed air, maintenance-grade facility lighting, tugs, jacks, safety equipment and shelter from the elements.

The maintenance team needs access to communications (internet), computers to access computer-based maintenance programs, access to technical data, i.e., technical publications, drawings, parts listings, and specific maintenance information to assist in troubleshooting and diagnostics. Maintenance technicians need continuous and recurrent training through the OEM maintenance training provider. The Aviation leader should review the maintenance overall capability through the same process; does the maintenance team have the resources, time, information, and training to do their jobs.

Not only is maintenance important on the systems and the aircraft under the inspection panels, the aircraft has to present itself so that a passenger that is not an Aviation professional, can look at the aircraft with limited or common knowledge (think of a vehicle that obviously appears to not be maintained, like the vehicles seen on the highway where is doubtful that it could ever pass even the most lenient inspection), would anyone feel comfortable climbing aboard the aircraft based on the things that they can see?

Cleaning an aircraft is part of the inspecting and maintained an aircraft process. The more contact time spent cleaning, the more likely a component prematurely wearing will be noticed, leaks can be found before they grow into a failure, corrosion, cracks, dents, distortions – all have a better chance of being found during a thorough post-mission cleaning process than a periodic inspection at a remote facility.

The aircraft Line Service Technicians may not be Aviation Airframe and Powerplant Technicians, but they have experience looking after the fleet's aircraft, they will know what is different because they'll see the same aircraft, the same landing gear and the same components dozens of times each month that they can be the first line of defense in a preventative maintenance program by identifying the wear patterns and changes in the appearance of the aircraft's specific components.

The Line Service Technician supports refueling, restocking, cargo and baggage handling/loading, aircraft cleaning and interior soft good conditioning and small repairs. And they help to maintain the aircraft in a like-new condition. An Aviation leader has the responsibility to care for and maintain the aircraft and equipment that they are responsible for within the standards identified by the organization. Maintenance and reliability are the critical priorities of the Aviation leader, but if the aircraft looks good and flies good, generally the maintenance status and program management speak for itself.

The Aviation Chief of Maintenance is one of the cornerstones of the Aviation organization. A stereotype exists and it is apparent when the Aviation Maintenance Chief speaks. It is a no non-sense personality that is slightly pessimistic, defined by if nothing is breaking, it is about to. If nothing is leaking, time to look closer. If the Dispatch Reliability Rate is beyond expectations, then the downturn will happen soon. The good Aviation Maintenance Technicians have spent time in the trenches, on the flight-line, troubleshooting, repairing, and getting aircraft back in the air. One thing they'll never do is compromise their integrity. A good maintenance technician knows without a doubt the status of their aircraft. They'll know what parts were changed and when, they know the top five maintenance issues for the fleet better than they know family birthdays and anniversaries. And when they say that the aircraft is fully mission capable, there is no need to doubt. It can be written in stone. A good Aviation Maintenance Chief will never compromise safety or reliability and would stake his oath on the correct status of the aircraft always. The downside is that political correctness may not be a strength and they will call it like they see it. If an Aviation Maintenance Chief like that is in the Aviation organization, don't let them leave. They are worth their weight in any precious metal. They are strong and unbending and that is exactly what it takes to have that title. They normally are the first in and the last to leave. The aircraft are theirs and the organization just gets to borrow them. Heaven helps the crewmember or maintenance technician that doesn't respect that.

The Aviation leader is also responsible for tracking costs of aircraft maintenance to determine what the most economical aircraft model design or even specific aircraft in the fleet. It's important to be able to track what costs are associated with a specific aircraft. Anything that would touch the aircraft should be included in the cost ledger. Repair parts, fuel, maintenance contact time, supplies, oil, oxygen systems refills… any of those items should be included in the ledger that the Aviation chief of maintenance uses to track and account for the costs of the aircraft. That total would simply be the total cost of the aircraft for maintenance and maintenance support. With that information it is easy to determine the actual cost per flying hour for that aircraft based on the number of hours that you've flown in that time. In the simplest terms, it is just running tally or ledger of costs. Even corrections can be accounted for if there is a warranty item that you can claim, for example, if a repair part was $1000 and you received warranty credit or a prorated credit on repair parts of maintenance, that is entered into the ledger as a credit. But the importance thing is, make sure that each cost is accounted for so that it is easy to track the total cost of maintenance for each aircraft through its lifetime of service.

Aviation organizations try to make the most efficient use out of their maintenance time and maintenance is normally done on the aircraft that is not scheduled for flight or is not required to be scheduled or operational.

Normally a progressive maintenance schedule is used, and the FAA devised a maintenance program years ago that allowed manufacturers to create maintenance programs that would be progressive and so the aircraft is in maintenance and undergoing inspections when time permits. Any part replacement or maintenance is scheduled when time permits. The Aviation organization minimizes the downtime for scheduled inspections and component replacements. This opportunity allows less impact to overall mission reliability and increases the overall dispatch rate of the aircraft by allowing more flight time and less scheduled maintenance time. It is most important that the times are tracked, and the organization knows the overall mission reliability rate. That is a key metric, and it is simply how often were you able to support scheduled missions as opposed to when they had to cancel or even when they were delayed.

Tracking the overall mission rate allows an organization to determine the success of mission accomplishment for the organization but it does little to track what the operational rate or the dispatch rate is for each aircraft.

For that metric, tracking the dispatch rate is normally determined by noting when the aircraft is scheduled to fly and when it doesn't fly that affects the overall dispatch rate. The Aviation organizations maintenance chief plays a critical role on making sure the aircraft are available when needed and mission ready. That is the critical and primary responsibility. Additional duties for the Aviation maintenance chief and his section that includes facilities maintenance and field operations.

In summary, Aviation maintenance chiefs' responsibilities are mission reliability, dispatch reliability for each aircraft and overall reliability when compared to the OEM's tracked metric for that specific model of aircraft. The Aviation maintenance chief also tracks and knows the costs associated with each aircraft. It is also necessary for the Aviation maintenance chief to track all associated maintenance costs, reliability rates, flying hours cycles, communications fees, subscriptions, and anything that adds costs to the aircraft and impacts the cost per flying hour.

Tracking this data allows the Aviation organization the ability to attribute costs to specific tail numbers. In turn, this allows the organization to identify and determine the total cost of the aircraft and the aircraft overall dispatch rate or operational rate.

If the rate falls below the rate of the organization's fleet average or below the overall manufactures average number for the aircraft fleet average, it allows decisions to be made that would improve the reliability rates or determine if the aircraft has reached its economic life based on maintenance costs and reliability. Software tracking systems are available to maintain the information, but a simple accounting ledger and maintenance tracking system that tracks both costs and reliability is what is needed.

Chapter Twelve – The Conduct of the Flight – Care and Feeding of Your Passengers and Cargo

As mentioned previously, air travel does several things great, but the most valuable product for air travel is saving time. Aviation operations should have a decided advantage over every other form of transportation when compared against any other form of travel. Otherwise, the passengers will ask the question of why they are paying for a luxury that should be part of the product when the time savings aren't apparent. Anyone that is perceptive enough to watch birds fly should be able to deduce that this flying form of transportation is fast, in fact, it is the fastest. There are thousands of examples of why it isn't that way, all one needs to do is look closely at schedules… Flying from Pittsburgh to Washington DC sounds like a great solution until a closer review of the schedule.

The following is not for Aviation professionals so please bypass this example... (it's a little basic, but helpful)

Look at this example:

A passenger would like to travel to Washington, D.C. from Pittsburgh for business. Just like millions of people around the world, the passenger goes to his smart phone app and gets the information. There are two commercial airports in Washington, D.C.: Washington Reagan and Washington Dulles. If I wanted to go into Washington Reagan, the flight time listed on the schedule is 3 hours, 33 minutes by way of Newark, NJ. Giving the benefit of doubt here that most know a little about the geography of the United States and that Newark is north and east of DC... so there is already a little disadvantage. Plus, the aircraft stops in Newark... Does anyone really want to go to Newark when the actual destination is DC? With any geographically savvy in mind, that route probably isn't the first choice from Pittsburgh if any knowledge of geography comes to bear on the decision. Given that, the next option is Pittsburgh to Dulles. Direct flight from Pittsburgh to Dulles, about an hour. From airport to airport is about an hour. Not many people officially live at airports, so there is the travel time from wherever to the airport. So, here's where geography also comes into the discussion; if traveling from the west of a north-south line bisecting Pittsburgh, you're going to have to add that travel time to your overall decision. If you are east of that line, you are closer to your destination. Assume that the drive time from the west is one-hour and from the east one-hour. (This is oversimplified, since north and south also comes into account.) The drive from Washington Dulles optimistically is about 35-minutes. So far, living east of Pittsburgh one-hour, one-hour flight, 35-minute drive is about two-hours and 35-minutes from start point to destination, add another optimistic hour for airport check-in... total travel time is about three hours and 35-minutes. The ground travel distance by road is four hours, 15-minutes to cover a circuitous route of 241 statute miles. The straight-line distance from Pittsburgh Airport to Dulles Airport is 158 statute miles. The aircraft trip from Pittsburgh to Washington took an optimistic three hours and 35-minutes elapsed time to fly, which was an average speed of 51 miles per hour. Driving the circuitous distance of 241 miles and arriving in four hours and 15 minutes is an average speed was 57 miles per hour. So, 51 miles per hour by jet aircraft and 57 miles per hour by most any automobile. Seems illogical, but it isn't. Compare costs – the average plane ticket costs four times as much as a rental car charge. So, we deduce that we are costing more to travel slower... (see Mr. Elon Musk's quote at the beginning of the chapter to understand why Aviation has to do it faster and better, because we cannot do it cheaper.)

Reducing ground travel times, minimizing airport dead time, flying as direct as possible and taking advantage of the speeds that aircraft has, gives Aviation the advantage. Aviation professionals, regardless of the type of organization they are part of, must be cognizant of that fact – otherwise the advantage that Aviation has over other forms of transportation begins to diminish. Safe, secure, and efficient (efficient as defined by many parameters including getting to the destination faster than other forms of transportation) is the objective in Aviation.

Start with the passenger and define the start point and the destination. Where are the nearest airports that can support the operations of the aircraft. Keep in mind the road network as well as traffic, stops, detours, and trafficability. From the time travel starts, what is the shortest distance in terms of time from the start point to the airport. Minimize airport ground time. Think five giant steps. Stepping from one form of transportation to another and getting within five giant steps of the other mode saves travel time. Dropping off from the ground conveyance at the aircraft is as short as it gets. Baggage loading should take no more than the time it takes for passengers to board, sit down and settle in. Briefings, engine starts can be simultaneous. Taxiing will be the largest variable. Flying direct and fast should be the objective. Once on the ground, efficiencies should be the same; aircraft to ground transportation, route to destination determined, stop the clock. The goal should be to have the elapsed time less than what it takes for ground conveyance. For longer distances traveled the time-savings should be exponential since there is more in-air travel time to take advantage of aircraft speeds and direct routing.

The key is anticipating, planning, and executing and the Aviation Operations Team does this better than any other organization. The Aviation Operations team starts with the departure point of the passenger(s), consider fastest form of ground transportation, closest airports, time loading, starting, taxiing, taking off, flying, landing, taxiing, unload times, ground transportation times and arrival at the destination. Sometimes referred to as door-to-door travel time, the objective is to build a repeatable process that does that quickly, safely, securely, and efficiently.

That's the objective, now how is it done – it's done by looking at each step of travel and looking at how to save time.

Time saving is the reason Aviation is selected. But it doesn't end there. Now that we have our passengers and cargo, there must be a deliberate process in place to exceed their expectations toward the care and literal feeding of the passengers. Going back to the Aviation Personality Type discussion, Aviation professionals should be just that, professionals. They want to be part of an organization that does the one thing that they are tasked to do better than anyone else. The discussion really starts with that attitude, regardless of the Aviation Organization Type and the appropriately-paired Aviation Personality Type – the minimum standard of service is continuous improvement for the organization and the individuals on the team. Every individual needs to challenge themselves and compare themselves to how they did it the last time... was there a desire for continuous improvement until perfection was attained (which is probably never, but that is the goal for which we aim). For the purposes of this chapter, that is the starting point.

Each member of the team knows their role. And each should strive to exceed the expectations toward time-savings, care and feeding.

Now that the right people are in the right place, designing the process is easy.

1. Aviation Operations receives the mission request, including the departure point street address for the passenger(s) departing and the destination street address for the passenger(s).
2. Ground transportation is arranged. If internal, ground transportation operators are the professional given the task to save time on that segment of travel. If external, Aviation operations reviews the plan and verifies the efficiency of the plan.
3. The airport facility is designed to provide and efficient flown of transfer between ground and air modes of travel. (Think five-giant steps as the optimum efficiency, where less is better.) Driveways, stopping

points, people and cargo transfer process, security gates, positioning of aircraft – every part of the process should be deliberately reviewed to minimize time on the ground.

4. Ground Aviation staff – security officers, people and cargo handlers, maintenance team, cabin crewmembers and flight deck crew need to plan, rehearse, and know the process to minimize ground time. Processes are developed and checklists are designed to get the timing down to pit crew like synergies and efficiencies. The clock starts when passengers step out of the departure door and walk into the arrival door.

5. On-Board – cabin crew has seats prepped, food and service items set out as planned, briefings prepared, right down to staging the coat hanger so that no extra steps are needed.

6. Flight Deck – mandatory documents (may be contained in the DOC Book) on board (Certificate of Airworthiness, Registration, Weight and Balance, Flight Plans, Weather and NOTAM briefing, Radio license, Operators Manual, manifests),preflight completed, checklist completed to the appropriate point in time, safety assessment checklists completed and acknowledged (any hazards are mitigated and discussed with the Aviation organization leadership and mitigation

strategies discussed), aircraft refueled, staged on the ready-line, gate, or hot-spot, APU/ground power connected, cabin powered, illuminated, temperature comfortable, run-up or pre-start checklist completed, weather data received, guidance systems programmed, seats/seatbelts adjusted, headsets connected, tested, volumes adjusted, cockpit lighting adjusted, checklists completed to engine start. Flight deck and crew briefings completed, final walk-around completed (aircraft brakes set, pins and covers pulled, chocks pulled if safe, external doors latched and secured – last remaining action to load baggage, close doors, load passengers, close doors and inspected for properly latching. Minimum showtime 90-minutes for domestic, 120-minutes for international if not duty-day restricted. All aircraft duties completed in 45-minutes, crew briefing conducted at 45—minutes prior to scheduled departure, prepared for passenger arrival 30-minutes prior to arrival… reviewing weather, taxi routes, takeoff and departure plan and emergency actions, check for de-icing if applicable to name just a few of the details.

7. Tracking – knowing the whereabouts of your passengers when you have that responsibility is essential. The goal is to provide safe, secure, efficient air transportation and exceeding the expectations. Knowing when ground

transportation is on site waiting for passengers, when the aircraft is in position and ready for passengers is critical. Having a contingency plan in place to keep passengers within the timeline of the well-planned schedule is also part of anticipating that if something goes wrong, there is also a plan in place to get everything back on track. There is nothing better than having a plan go awry and having a ready-made plan to get things back on track, especially if it is known in advance that potential problems are ahead. As passenger reach critical milestones on the travel plan; pick from departure point, clearing anticipated high-density traffic areas, two-minutes away may sound un-necessary but if you have planned it well, anticipated potential problem areas and have alternatives in place, then you're performing at the expected level of professionalism. Operations planning cycle always includes anticipating, and anticipating means knowing the things that are on the critical path to success and planning around them. Busy airports, busy cities, slot times, customs clearance delays… all very possible and likely in the world of Aviation. If the potential is known, then the contingency should be planned. A few simple "what-if's" are all anyone needs to ask. If it was anticipated and thought of as a possibility, then the reasonable answer is to answer the "what-if" question. Keeping track of your passengers as they pass critical points in the plan allows the team to continue to be ahead of a decision cycle and work through the contingencies. All of this is well within the capability of a well-trained and experienced Aviation operations team. Normally there are non-Aviation folks that may work with passengers and schedules. If you keep in the back of your mind that they are not Aviation professional, that will help you work through some of the self-imposed issues that cause problems. Schedules that are built around adherence to an estimated flight time across the north Atlantic, and allow for zero slack time for all of the miles that have to be crossed need contingencies and beg the question of what happens if the weather is not as forecasted and the aircraft is delayed in arrival holding for 30-minutes, or if the aircraft holds and then diverts – is the contingency plan in place and has it been communicated to the passengers. In a perfect world, everything goes according to plan, in the real-world contingencies need to think through and ready to be put in place with no or minimal disruption. Know the status of where the passengers are according to the plan and be ready to adjust to put things back on track, including communications to everyone that is affected by a change.

8. Plan the flight and fly the plan – The Aircraft Captain has the regulatory responsibility to conduct the flight and keep everyone on the aircraft safe. Federal Aviation Regulation Part 91-3 gives the Aircraft Captain, the Pilot-in-Command direct responsibility and is the final authority for the safe conduct of the flight. <u>A passenger has no right to interfere with that duty, in fact it is illegal, and punishment is defined at the Federal level.</u> With that level of responsibility, the Aircraft Captain must make sure that everything and everyone is safe and not creating an unsafe situation. Everything is within the scope of that regulation and anything that prevents safe conduct of the flight is reason enough for a delay or flight cancellation due to a safety factor that has been determined by the Pilot-In-Command. Aircraft Captains should conduct themselves and be the best example of professionalism in Aviation. The aircraft Captain is directly responsible for the success of the mission.

Chapter Thirteen – Aircraft and Passenger Security... is a Sub-Set of Safety

A safety incident is an unintended event that brings harm to the passengers, crew, or aircraft. A security incident is an intended event that harms the passengers, crew, or aircraft.

If either happens, a safety or security incident, the chances of mission success are not good. Remember the requirements of the mission – conduct safe, secure, efficient aviation operations while exceeding the expectations. A safety or security incident that harms the passengers, crew or aircraft violate the mission statement.

Security is part of the mission preparation process – anticipating, planning, and executing. Prevent safety and security incidents by in-depth planning. Identify potential risks to safety and security – they exist. Services exist that collect aviation specific intelligence and can brief the Aviation operations and flight crew team on what threats exist to security depending on the area or destination. Countermeasures should be determined by the security and operations team working together and developing the security plan at the airport and if Aviation operations is coordinating it, the security vulnerabilities of the ground transportation plan. As part of the Aviation safety briefing, include the Aviation security briefing in order to prevent unintended and intended harm from coming to passengers, crew, and aircraft.

Chapter 14 – Conduct of the Flight

Do everything necessary to make flight safe, secure, and efficient while exceeding the expectation.

There are hundreds of thousands of requirements that go into making the previous statement happen. Everyone in the Aviation organization has a personal responsibility to ensure that happens.

It is the duty of the Aviation leader to make it happen every single time an aircraft takes to the air.

Whatever it takes to fly safely is what must be done!

Chapter Fifteen - Base of Operations, Hangar Facilities, Support Areas, and Remote Operations Away from the Base of Operations

The Aviation Base of Operations is the home of the Aviation organization. It is the location where all the support is located. Everything from hangars to office space, tools to technology, and everything that gives the Aviation organization the shelter and location for everything that it needs.

The Hangar is the centerpiece of the Aviation organization's base of operations. To be an effective base of operations, it needs to have the following:

- Sufficient area to house the Aviation organizations aircraft and sufficient room to allow for movement in and out (with remote control tug equipment, ground handling is safer since the operator can stop, reposition to a vantage point to ensure clearance)

- The hangar floor area lighting should meet aircraft maintenance level lighting standards and provide bright illumination to show true colors as well as minimize shadows.
- The hangar floor area should be large enough to allow ground support equipment to be placed near the aircraft, including power carts, portable HVAC systems, hydraulic mules, avionics test equipment and tools.
- Hangars should have storage areas for tools, toolboxes, ground support equipment
- Hangars should have overhead lift capability installed or available, air compressors, fall protection and OSHA safety equipment (eye wash stations, first aid kits, AEDs, firefighting equipment and evacuation route plans posted)
- Shop areas should provide enough space for safe clearances between special tool stations, vent hood, benches with test equipment, work benches for small component work and packaging components for shipment to OEMs or repair facilities.
- Storage areas for cabin service items, food, and beverages for aircraft service

- Commissary area (enclosed room) with refrigeration, storage cabinets, shelving, and facilities for catering and perishable food item storage
- Storage areas for aircraft spares and components (tires and wheels, cabin spare carpets, bedding, fly away gear)
- Laundry facilities
- Locker rooms, showers, rest rooms, uniform storage for maintenance clothing (maintenance team clothing should be from a uniform service company that can launder maintenance clothing so that hazardous material contamination and corrosive agents are not contaminating employee homes and laundry facilities)
- Separate storage or annex for maintenance stands, luggage carts, hydraulic mules, tugs, additional GSE, hangar maintenance equipment, ladders, and generators)
- If ground vehicles are to be stored inside the hangar facility, safety would suggest that there is a robust firewall between the ground vehicles and the aircraft for fire safety, inadvertent ground vehicle – aircraft collisions, and FOD (tires can pick up a variety of bits and pieces in the tire treads)
- Maintenance Team office space should have separate HVAC systems and ventilation systems separate from the hangar HVAC and ventilation systems.

- Hazardous waste should be stored outside of the area where aircraft are stored and separated from battery service areas, charging areas with robust firewalls and standoff distance so that an ignition source and fuel are not co-located.
- Hangar structures should be designed and approved for the environment, areas that receive snowfall should be structurally sufficient to withstand snow roof loads, hangars in coastal areas should be stressed to withstand high wind loads typical for the environment.
- Hangars need to be sized for the type of aircraft and number of aircraft.
- Hangars need to have backup power supplies that run independently from the commercial power source and provide sufficient continuous power to sustain activities within the facility.
- Aviation operations work areas should have visibility or monitors for driveways, ramp areas and hangar floor areas, provide sufficient office space for the number of operations specialists employed per shift, have office lighting that meets design standards, power access, network and communications access, radio connections for direct ground to air communications using standard aircraft VHF frequencies.

- Break areas should have monitors, lighting that meets breakroom standards, refrigerators, tables chairs, dishwashers, sinks, microwaves, storage cabinets, windows to the outside, doors for noise and environmental control.
- Kitchen area for food service preparation scaled to the demand for the organization.
- Office areas for support staff with sufficient space to allow work areas, personal item storage, computers, telephones, monitors, lighting to meet design standards, windows to the outside, doors for noise, environmental and security controls.
- Common office areas with printers, paperwork production supplies, paper shredders, trash bins, including recyclables, storage cabinets, tables, windows, and lighting to meet design standards.
- Hangars should be well insulated for environmental as well as noise control.
- Observation areas to view ramp areas and airport operating environments.
- Covered parking areas for ground side parking sufficient for daytime work population.
- Security fencing that meets TSA security standards and security systems or security officers that are sufficient to protect high value assets.

- Exterior lighting that meets design standards for ramp, driveway, and doorway areas
- Questions normally develop about meeting ADA or mobility requirements, for Aviation personnel this normally is answered by the medical screening that is consistent with ensuring people are hired with the physical and mental abilities to meet the job requirements, for example; pilots have medical certificate requirements, cabin crew have mobility and physical ability to lift certain amounts overhead and assist in aircraft evacuations, maintenance technicians have physical ability requirements so normally the job requirements will ensure that Aviation personnel have the physical abilities to walk the distances from parking areas, climb stairs, and navigate buildings that are designed with a minimum design requirement that meets the ADA requirements. Most new facility designs will meet these standards, however older facilities may have to be retrofitted to allow for minor ADA accommodations.

Note: The hangar should be designed, built, and maintained to a standard that attracts Aviation team members and a place where it has all that is needed to do their work, and be a place where they enjoy spending their time. The facilities will usually fall in line and be appropriate for the type of aviation organization.

Chapter Sixteen - Assessment and Audits – How Do You Know Your Good

Inspections, reviews, and discussions are all designed to review critical functions and provide feedback on how well the Aviation organization is doing when compared to a measurable standard. Here are some of the audits, reviews, and inspections that most Aviation organizations should expect and be prepared to facilitate routinely *(please note that this is not a comprehensive list but an outline of what types an Aviation organization can or should expect)*:

> Federal Aviation Administration certification audits or inspections – most Federal Aviation Regulations (FAR) Part 91 operations have minimal requirements for an FAA audit but nonetheless should always be prepared.

FAR Part 121,125,135, 91K operations should expect this routinely and unannounced conducted by FAA personnel.

- International Standards for Business Aircraft Operations (IS-BAO) – is a comprehensive safety standard audit and registered organizations receive certification that is recognized by countries and entities around the world. IS-BAO has standard audit protocols for initial and reoccurring audits completed by IS-BAO accredited auditor.
- Flight Safety Foundation (FSF) – has safety standards that prescribes recommended procedures for safe flight operations this is normally completed by the Aviation organizations Safety Officer or Manager using the prescribed protocols recommended by FSF.
- Financial Audits – normally complete by the organization or for certain Aviation organizations an external auditor for different financial purposes. This audit is something that the Aviation leader should insist on happening routinely, especially in non-Aviation profession organizations. Aviation is a high-cost endeavor and routine audits ensure transparency, accountability and compliance with internal policies, IRS and SEC requirements.

- Internal Safety Audits – normally conducted by organizational safety departments that utilize checklists and require procedures that may or may not include Aviation specific requirements or realize that many Aviation practices have hierarchical regulatory requirements that limit local policy applicability.
- Flight Standards Checks – normally required by the flight crews to meet the Federal Aviation Administration requirements outlined in the Code of Federal Regulations, Title 14. The Aviation organization Chief of Standards or Chief Pilot normally has the responsibility delegated by the Aviation leader to ensure that pilots and flight deck crew members are following the Federal Aviation Regulations (FARs). There is an exhaustive list of regulatory requirements covered in Title 14 for Aviation operations. The list below does not cover them all but for the non-Aviation professional, it provides an example of the strict regulatory environment in which Aviation organizations operate:
    - Part 61.57 Recent Flight Experience
    - Part 61.58 Proficiency Requirements
    - Part 61.59 Fabrication of Records
    - Part 91.3 Responsibility and Authority of the Pilot in Command
    - Part 91.11 Illegal to Threaten Flight Crews

- Part 91.117 Aircraft Speed
- Part 91.119 Minimum Safe Altitude
- Part 91.121 Altimeter Settings
- Part 91.137 TFRs and Disaster Areas
- Part 91.151 Fuel Requirements
- Part 91.167 Fuel Requirements for Instrument Flight
- Part 91.169 Instrument Flight Weather Minimums

- Cabin Crew Standards Checks – normally complete by the Cabin Crew Chief periodically to ensure that all cabin crew members comply with the standards, policy, and regulatory requirements for flight operations. The requirements vary depending on the aircraft Certificate of Airworthiness.

- Security Audits – normally completed by the TSA or authorized organization to provide training and policy documents, contact numbers and general information, especially of the Aviation organization has a security requirement to maintain. In the United States, the highest level of recognized security protocols is contained in the requirements to access the Washington National Reagan Airport (KDCA) and is defined by the requirements listed in the District of Columbia Airport Standard Security Program (DASSP). The DASSP program was developed by the TSA shortly after September 11th to ensure that Part 91, 91K, and 135 certificated operators had a means to verify that security standards were met, recognized and authorization granted for operations into sensitive security areas. While access to DCA is normally not widely required, access to the US National Airspace System (NAS) is shared by all. In the event of a critical situation like what happened on September 11th, 2001, where aircraft were grounded and prevented from air operations, the DASSP program will hopefully allow compliant operators to receive authorization to operate in the NAS quickly by using the protocols that transmit authorization to operators like the process used for access into Washington Reagan Airport. The National Business Aircraft Association (NBAA) and General Aviation Manufactures Association (GAMA) was very instrumental in working with the newly established Transportation Security Administration (TSA) and US Secret Service (USSS) to develop the program that was implemented early after September 11th.

Chapter 17 - Records Keeping

Aviation organizations are highly regulated and operate within a very specific and unbreakable set of physical laws. Non-Aviation professionals may discuss thinking "outside of a box" and looking for new ways to make Aviation operations cheaper, faster, and better. To the Aviation professional these discussions are likely to elicit comments that aren't easily shared in polite society. There are many-thousands of examples of why thinking outside of the regulatory and physical law "box" just isn't practical because Aviation is strictly regulated, and the laws of physics will always trump what appears to be a rational argument to the non-Aviation professional.

Maintaining records in an Aviation organization is normally a requirement to comply with regulations and policies.

Here is an example of what records need to be maintained and audit or inspection ready always (highly over-simplified checklist):

- Financial records – anytime any of the organization's money is spent, there needs to be a record of who, what, why, when, where and how it was approved.
- Training records – anytime there is training happening, record who, what, why, when, where and how.
- Flight records – anytime an aircraft is flown, record who (crew and passengers), where, when, why, how and for what. What systems is used to keep flight, crew, and passenger records, including cost information for proxy statements, Internal Revenue Service (IRS), and Securities Exchange Commission (SEC) reporting as well as compensation for imputed income.
- Maintenance record - on anything that needs to be maintained – especially aircraft, ground vehicles, facilities, air compressors, HVAC systems – if it mechanical, it needs to be maintained and it needs to be recorded with who, what, where, when, why and how.
- Fuel and Energy Consumption – who, where, when, how much, why, what
- People records – anything pertaining to people; Aviation team members, passengers, support staff (organic and external)

- And the records keeping process, how is it completed, accessed and secured, who is responsible for maintaining the record, where is it stored, what do we want to record and why do we do it – there is always a reason, and someone will ask what that reason is – have an answer.

Chapter 18 - Tradition and Progress

Aviation has been around in various forms since 400 BC when kites were flown and gave man the idea for human flight. On December 17th, 1903, the Wright Brothers proved their design worked after they studied, designed, developed, tested and successfully flew the Wright flyer.

Since those times and throughout our modern era, we have flown billions of passenger miles with an enviable safety record considering the inherent dangers of the endeavor. Aviation is the safest way travel and that credit goes directly to every one of the professionals involved, the regulators, the aircraft manufacturers, the pilots, the cabin crew, the maintainers, the operations planners and the ground support staff all work together within a proven system of verification, checklists, safety protocols and processes that are proven and have evolved over the years to be one of the safest and most sustainably safe processes anywhere today.

It works mainly due to the process inherent in the system, by passing on the experiences of thousands of people and taking the opportunity to be very deliberate and leery of changes. It must be that way. Every process and every tradition in Aviation is normally the result of an exhaustive root-cause analysis and system that gets information to the people and organizations that need the information.

So, the traditional methods of Aviation are proven. Each and every regulation, process, policy, procedure, and checklist are the result of a finding and exhaustive, deliberate study to find the one and only right answer.

The great news is that we don't have to know the details of why everything is in place the way it is, because there is a process that discovers, investigates, and resolves issues. Hundreds of thousands of people are working in Aviation to allow all Aviation professionals to take advantage of the findings.

The bottom line here is that while we may not know all the details. We know that whatever has happened and however the process works, it works.

All Aviation professionals must do is to tap into that astounding process and gain knowledge from it.

Honor the traditions because they work and regardless of who or how, resist the temptation to change something that has been in place and produces results.

Every change in Aviation brings about unintended consequences. Many people have unknowingly blundered into oblivion by being smarter than the engineers and pilots that have written the procedures and the checklists.

Aviation is an evolutionary process that accepts change through exhaustive study and research where every small step of research and testing done deliberately move safety further along to decrease accidents and prevents injury or death.

Aviation is a trusted and sacred profession. A pilot of an aircraft holds the lives of the crew and passengers in their skilled hands. There is a time for jovialness and light-heartedness, but never should it be during a time where credibility and judgmental abilities can be questioned.

The pilot standards of conduct should be exactly the standards of the highest professional, in actions, deeds words and dress, especially during an initial or public meeting.

Please know that the world may have changed, but human expectations have not.

Anyone worth their salt, is paying close attention to whomever is holding their lives in their hands. When in doubt, fall back on traditions – that will never steer a true professional wrong. The pilot standards of a white shirt, tie, pressed trousers, jacket, shined shoes, clean shaven personal grooming is a visual display that personal attention to details and decisiveness translates to conduct in a critical event or safety sensitive endeavor. (Ever try to seal an oxygen mask at 41,000 feet with a mustache and beard? – there is a reason why that standard, just like everything else is a deliberate act in Aviation.)

Whatever process may be in place, ask before changing. Observe what has worked and delivers safe results continuously.

While the world seems to be turning itself on end, Aviation must resist radical and revolutionary change. Everything from entry standards into flight schools for basic aptitude to medical standards have all have the origins in lessons learned and a system that continuously produces safe, secure, and efficient air travel. Aviation professionals are the keeper of the standards, and they are in place because someone paid for the improvement with their life. Study the reasons, the traditions, and the process.

Be sure to improve it as an Aviation professional rather than upend it! It is the Aviation leader's responsibility to uphold the Aviation standards to keep our sacred profession trusted and valued.

Chapter 19 - Aviation Organizations and Associations

There are many Aviation centric organizations that have the collective experience of hundreds of thousands, if not millions, of Aviation professionals that have provided information, worked on committees, served on Boards and continue the discussion around all subjects Aviation. In terms of collaboration, there are excellent and credible Aviation professional organizations that exist to bring Aviation professionals together to solve the challenges and problems that are common to every Aviation professional, everywhere.

Here are just a few organizations that have been a credible source of Aviation information sharing. Review the programs and information that they have to offer in advance so that when challenges are presented, the information and source credibility are readily available.

1. The National Business Aircraft Association (NBAA) nbaa.org
2. The Flight Safety Foundation (FSF) flightsafety.org
3. General Aviation Manufacturers Association (GAMA) gama.aero
4. Cessna Pilots Association (CPA) cessna.org
5. Overseas Security Advisory Council (OSAC) www.osac.gov
6. Aircraft Owners and Pilots Association (AOPA) www.aopa.org
7. International Business Aircraft Council ibac.org
8. National Air Transportation Association www.nata.aero

If there were only a few that you have time to support, please consider supporting the NBAA, IBAC, FSF and GAMA. There are many more, but since there isn't enough time to support everyone, these three offer the most returns on the investment of time and money.

Chapter 20 – Aviation Envy – Yes, it is a Real Hurdle

In retrospect, it is easy to understand why Aviation envy is a hurdle to overcome. If the phrase, "if you pursue a career that you are passionate about, and are successful, you'll never work a day in your life" is true, then Aviation professionals that pursued Aviation as a career path have the market cornered. Everyone has met people that dreamed of careers in Aviation, but many claim that they were limited by physical requirements, aptitude capabilities or not knowing that such a fantastic profession is possible or how to get into it.

Every Aviation professional has experienced the comments that are both complimentary and envy filled at the same time. It shouldn't be a factor in the life of adults, but human emotions are just as consistent as the lift/drag equation. In fact, applying the same calculations in gauging the envy factor may be just as consistent. There is no doubt that Aviation professionals understand the mystique about being a professional in the field of Aviation, but those not as familiar as to why there is that mystic will never understand.

Aviation envy is an important topic to understand from a non-Aviation professional's perspective since there are many ways that Aviation envy may influence support decisions.

Aviation is expensive – not many people really understand why organizations spend so much to support the Aviation organization especially if it is not within an Aviation organization. It's a difficult concept to understand when cost relativity is concerned. Imagine an accountant processing an invoice for a single repair part for an aircraft that is greater than their annual salary, especially when it comes time for budget reductions. Imagine how a manager feels for another department within the same organization about salary when they discover that a pilot or maintenance technician makes just as much or more, and they are the profit center for the organization and Aviation a cost center. Imagine that 99% of the non-Aviation organization must fly coach when the top 1% fly's in abject luxury beyond anything that they can dream of... If this starts to paint a picture, then it is easy to see why Aviation draws the wrath of the masses that are not able to participate in the process or ability that Aviation has to offer. In the military, imagine an infantryman living in primitive conditions watching military aircraft overhead and knowing that things like food, lodging, adequate rest, and exercise are part of the fatigue mitigation strategy. Imagine the talk around the break room or lunchroom when Aviation professionals are discussing the last trip to some exotic and tropical destination as a matter of routine, when some only plan a trip like that once in a lifetime.

Aviation is highly selective and experienced based – While it is difficult for Aviation professionals that have the "right stuff" to realize it, but there are hundreds of gates to pass through for an Aviation professional to earn their "coveted" wings. How many times have Aviation professionals discussed what they do for a living, and someone mentions that they wanted to get into Aviation, but their eyes were bad, or they had a hereditary health issue that prevented them from pursuing their dreams of Aviation. How many people have started working in Aviation but for some reason, timing or aptitude or self-imposed stresses prevented them from reaching their goals.

Crewing, scheduling, dispatching, maintaining, and flying aircraft is an amazing ability and to be able to say that you are in the Flight Department, or work for an Airline, or fly aircraft within the organization draws admiration and envy all at the same time. While Aviation professionals work in controlled, pristine, well-funded and perfect conditions, many other professions do not. When the overall budget for the organization is reduced and Aviation is spared because of the requirements of Aviation maintenance, training and support, everyone notices, and everyone has the same withdrawn comments – why are they so special.

Everything about Aviation is obscure to the non-Aviation professional. The seemingly expensive costs, the maintenance requirements, the support requirements, the training requirements are question marks in many non-Aviation professional's minds. But it is all reduced to that primitive human emotion of envy. "Why do they get to, and I don't?" Even the most educated and poised professional has it, but they may disguise it a little better.

How does and Aviation leader and professional manage this emotional reaction that has no basis in rationality?

The only answer that is feasible is to be aware that it exists and take measures to address it. While some are deep-rooted in their envy toward Aviation, they can at least be aware that Aviation provides a service that is difficult to attain elsewhere.

The Aviation leader should look for every opportunity within the organization to support the overall non-Aviation segments of the organization.

A friendly and humble approach can normally breakdown all barriers to communication and attitudes that promote the "untouchability" of Aviation professionals on widens the gap and increases the envy.

The Aviation leader should look and explore every opportunity to support the greater organization. If the top layer of management has access to aircraft, look for ways to support everyone.

Aviation organizations that employ shuttle aircraft to move every level of employee understand that the value may be equivalent to the other means of transportation, but the Flight Department is there to serve everyone within the organization and help make their lives better. Imagine that an organization based in the mid-west schedules an event on either coast. The top-level managers, leave the same day, attend the event and are back home for dinner. Never mind that those top level leaders are driving the profitability that everyone enjoys, the only thought from the 100 other employee is that the top ten percent is using Aviation efficiently and they had to leave days earlier and arrive home days later to attend the same event and their workload may not be as highly valued are the top ten percent, they still have the same amount of work to do and travel means late nights when they are back in the office or over the weekends.

Why not charter an aircraft or several aircraft to shuttle employees to offsite events. The happiness factor is increased, productivity is increased, airfare, hotel and rental car costs are reduced, and Aviation envy is reduced.

There are so many examples of how the Aviation leader can drive the same levels of travel efficiencies and work efficiencies into lower levels of the organization. The Aviation leader should, along with the organization's senior leader team, explore each, evaluate the cost-benefits and make a decision that truly takes care of people within the organization.

The Aviation leader needs to understand that this is a real issue and that it can affect everything from resources, information, time, and training abilities if it is not managed.

Being part of the organization, not just the people at the hangar that no one knows. The Aviation leader should constantly look for ways to leverage Aviation's benefits anywhere and everywhere within the greater organization and senior leaders should be keen to provide the opportunities to the greater organization as a whole.

Just knowing that this may exist creates the awareness and the awareness allows the Aviation leader to develop countermeasures only limited by his ability to draw parallels for the needs of the greater organization and the abilities of Aviation.

Within Aviation organization, is untapped abilities and capabilities that the Aviation leader and the senior leaders within the organization should be aware and prepared to leverage them toward any challenge that the organization may face.

Chapter 21 - Recognition and Rewards for the Aviation Professional

"We praise in public and admonish in private", is an important concept when it comes to taking care of Aviation professional. And there is no better way to praise in public by having awards and recognition programs that acknowledge favorable actions and provide public appreciation for a job well done. Periodic meetings and updates, such as quarterly updates, monthly safety meetings and other meetings such as town halls, mission briefings and other opportunities where the department, team or section is together. Aviation leaders should sponsor programs where senior leaders provide recognition and awards and acknowledge achievements. We certainly don't hesitate to call someone in to counsel for negative behaviors, why not take the same opportunity to select high levels of achievements.

Awards and rewards come in many forms and opportunities for recognition, and some can be confusing. Here is a list of common practices for acknowledging positive accomplishments:

1. Special Recognition Award – monetary awards from $25 or more to highlight accomplishments that have save the company money in a direct analysis. For the Aviation organization, a maintenance team shares in a $3,000 award for maintenance performed at the organization's facility that saved $30,000 in maintenance costs offsite and reduced downtime by 30%.

2. Safety Awards – Small gift, gift card for lunch or coffee that rewarded someone that prevented a condition that may have led to a reportable safety incident. Maybe an employee recommended installing no-slip floor covering in a hangar that was a frequent slip, trip or fall hazard area.

3. Leadership award plaque or engraving that highlighted an action or activity that positively influenced the Aviation organization. A pilot within the organization completed 500-hours of safe, secure, and efficient flight operations as the pilot in command of an aircraft. What a pleasure it is seeing those awards lined up in the organization's "wall of fame".

4. The organization's wings or lapel insignia with award indicators. Stars, diamonds, or numerical symbols that signify the number of hours for a pilot, number of safe maintenance events for a technician, number of years for an operations specialist, thousands of gallons dispensed by a refueler, and any other visible method that display the safe accomplishments of the team member.
5. Name recognition in newsletters, on-line info pages, or specific websites that recognize team members for positive actions and accomplishments.

However the reward or award takes shape, the Aviation leader should support activities that routinely recognizes the professionals with the Aviation organization. While no organization can adequately address the talents, skills, and abilities that the Aviation professional brings to the organization, any opportunity to show appreciation offers immeasurable returns. For the right Aviation Personality Type, the reward is not in the recognition, it is just being appreciated and the awards programs do the best that we can at that outside of normal, competitive salaries and benefits.

Chapter 22 - The Aviation Leaders New Assignment Assessment – the First 90-Days

Aviation professionals build foundations around their routines. Their routines are perfected by experience and what works.

A new Aviation leader's first 90-days are no different than any other leader's first actions, minimize changes and upsetting the routines that are successful. If there are routines that aren't successful in meeting the mission requirements, the new leader needs time to observe, identify, understand, evaluate, and determine opportunities to improves. The new Aviation leader should assume that the procedures, policies, and routines are working until proven otherwise, but that doesn't happen in a few hours or a few days. New leaders promoted within the organization normally come with a long list of when I am in charge, things will be different attitude. Before jumping into change from a previous perspective the new leader should again, observe, identify, understand, evaluate, and determine improvement opportunities based on the mission statement. Avoid making any changes unless they are safety related until you understand the standards, efficiencies, culture, social landscape, sensitivities and get to know area of operations for 90-days if your tours are expected to be more than two-years. Some leadership assignments may be less, especially in military and high-attrition units, but if you are new to the organization – observe and evaluate for at least 30-days before implementing changes. Any change should be directly connected to the mission statement (why are we making changes?) and to improving safety (no compromise on safety).

First steps.

1. People
2. Safety and Security
3. Operations
4. Logistics and Maintenance
5. Communications

The most important role for the new Aviation leader is to take time to get to know the Aviation professions that have the sacred task to accomplish the Aviation mission. This may come as a shock, but every other person in the Aviation organization is the expert in the organization. They know what works, what doesn't, what they need in terms of resources, time, training, and information. The new Aviation leader has to take the time to get to know each and every one, details matter! What motivates, what discourages, passions, center of gravity, pet peeves, birthdays (not age), family, spouses, children, concerns, fears, stress point… anything that give insight that allows the Aviation leader to better support them and get mission accomplished adds invaluable knowledge to the ability to motivate and get the job done right!

Week One through Three (the first 15-21 days)

1. Set up group meeting with the entire team in an offsite, neutral territory, social setting, The Aviation Ice-Breaker – the first official event should be a low threat, low stress, social activity where a brief introduction of the Aviation leader is all that is intended and next steps, discuss the elephant in the room, when and what is going to happen next and are there any impending changes. Discuss commitment, sharing, motivation, communication, appreciation, celebration. Listen to your team, exceed their expectations, manage costs and time as a valuable, finite resource, ask what should be done differently and what should stay the same.

2. Review the Mission Statement – who, what, how, where, when, and why. Understand what the Aviation organization does and its measure of success.

   Useful Documents to Gather:

   Mission Statement

   Previous Leaders Assessments

   Audit Results

3. Understand the organization structure, how is it currently structured to accomplish the mission. Draw out the organization chart and locate every member of the team in the organization chart by name, duty assignment and hierarchy.

   Useful Documents to Gather:

   The Organizational Chart

   Recall Rosters

   Team Rosters

   Team Schedules

4. Walk the Terrain – know the physical area of operations, facilities, support equipment, ramp space, aircraft.

Useful Documents to Gather:

Facilities maps

Equipment inventories

Aircraft inventories

Facilities work orders or repairs.

a. Review the inventor of assets or the property book (what physical assets the Aviation leader is responsible for)

b. Assess condition of the aircraft, RVSM, CPDLC, LOAs,

c. Set up meetings with tenant organizations, government leaders, ATC, ARFs, maintenance, FAA program manager.

d. What are the conditions of the facilities and take note of how well it is, or it isn't maintained and then find out the person responsible for that, good or bad?

e. What's the security like. Can anyone access the area, how is access controlled, who gets to touch the aircraft and how are they protected from tampering and damager – security cameras in place to observe areas.

5. Review the budget (operational and capital) with the Financial Business Partner

a. Total budget

b. Audits
c. Variances
d. Budgeting process
    i. Approving expenses
    ii. Approving invoices
    iii. Categories for budgeting

   Useful Documents to Gather:

   Organizational budget document

   Property book

   Lease agreements

   Master Support Agreements (training vendors, FSI, Simuflite, OEMs, Fuel suppliers, etc.)

   Letters of Agreement (FAA, Fire Station, Government organizations)

6. Meet with HR Business Partner - ask for any employee survey results, audits, reviews, evaluation results.
   Useful Documents to Gather:
       People rosters
       People performance reviews
       Medicals
       Special needs
       Standards Check rides.

Training records and qualifications
Pilot's licenses
Passports
Driver's licenses
Radio licenses (if needed)

7. Review written policies, procedures, evaluations, training records, adherence to training requirements, what are the standards defining documents (know them, understand them, and then assess – who meets, fails to meet, or exceeds the standards.
    a. Drug screening
    b. Medicals (who and where)
    c. Training requirements
    d. Inspections

    Useful Documents to Gather:
    Any and every policy document
    Authorization matrix
    Delegation of Authority
    Letters of Assignment
    Safety Affirmation from Key Leader

8. Meet with the subordinate leaders of the organization, know how they fit into the organization.

      a. know names, families, education, achievements, experiences, likes, dislikes, what is working well and where they see improvement. Determine their character and where they are on their personal and professional maturity scale. Assess complacency and seriousness.
9. Meet with every employee, understand where they fit within the organization.
      a. know names, families, education, experiences, achievements, likes, dislikes, what is working well and where they see improvement.

Week Four through Six (Day 16 through 37)

1. Observe the team doing their jobs, maintenance routines and events, operations planning, refueling, grounds maintenance, vehicle maintenance, flight operations. Look for as many opportunities to complete the assessment – use your standards teams and leaders to work with them. Ask hard questions that you already know the answer to assess accuracy and job knowledge. This phase of the assessment will take the most time as it needs to see the team in many of its operating environments.

Week Seven Through Nine (Day 35 through 63)

1. Begin assembling your assessment summary. The mission statement provides the objective, and the policies, procedures and standards provide the grade sheets.
2. Talk to leaders, let them know that this assessment is well-within the Aviation leader's area of expertise and that since they are the experts in the organization's abilities – ask questions. There are only three options; correct, incorrect and not knowing. When you are discussing the observations with the leader team – look specifically at the leaders that are defending wrong answers and how they defend them (remember, character assessment happens best when the person being observed is under stress.) Pay particular attention to defensiveness and excuses, look at the "push back" signals, when someone being challenged disengages and turns negative – probably a great indicator of true character. Look for leaders that pull closer to the table and offer ideas, not excuses. Try not to judge wrong or right – let the leaders do that. Once they have the realization that it was not the most efficient, then they'll jump and work to get it right. Be part of the team and remember, the Aviation leader sets the vision, defines the mission statement, and provides the information, resources, time and training to subordinate leaders to get

the job done within the standards defined by regulations, standards, policies, best-practices data and if none of that is available, gather data, assess and define the standards deliberately.

Aviation Right and Wrong Way Hierarchy

1. Regulations
2. Policies, Procedures, Standards and Routines defined in alignment with Regulations and Aviation best-practices.
3. Aviation Best practices
4. Internal data collection, review of how other Aviation organizations do it and are successful, assessments and implementation.

Aviation Standards Operating Procedures and Manuals

1. The "How To" manual that describes and defines how things are done within the Aviation Organization – The Manual

   (The manual is a compilation of those standards that have been deliberately determined as to how the Aviation organization will do things. It should be an evolving document that reflects the

hierarchical documents and re-states the guidance in a language that is clear, plain and understandable.

2. Adding, Deleting or Amending the Manual
    a. Create a new Operations Bulletin that prescribes how to get it done with clear, detailed language.
    b. The Operations Bulletin is distributed to everyone and becomes the temporary standards. The Operations Bulletin has a life span of 90-days. During that 90-days, it can be amended and rewritten. After the re-write the amended Operations Bulletin has a new life span of 90-days. And it continues that cycle until it has been proven as an effective way of how it is done.
    c. If the Operations Bulletin has not been amended in that 90-days and passes the test of supporting the mission safely, securely, and efficiently, the new procedure is added to the Operations Manual.

At the end of the review period, time to get to work. Compare the observations, determine what needs to be done to accomplish the mission. Review the status of the organization with the senior leader or principal of the greater organization and conduct a gap analysis. Prioritize corrective actions, document the findings and corrective actions, and build the get-well plan into individual objectives. The road to excellence begins with knowing what needs corrected or improved.

It is the continuous process that ends once perfection is attained.

Stay safe always and enjoy a profession that only the immortals once enjoyed.

You're defying gravity – you're flying – enjoy the best career that has ever existed!

Index

air travel, xvi, 57, 166, 170, 198
Aircraft Authorizer, 147
Aircraft costs, 67
Aircraft Requirements, xix, 56
Aircraft Selection Team, 109
airport facility, 171
American Interbank Offered Rate, 141
Attitudes are everything, 18
attributes of an experienced aircraft consultant, 110
Aviation centric organizations, 64, 200
Aviation Chief of Maintenance, 38, 161
Aviation consultant, 110, 111, 112, 113, 114, 115, 116, 121, 134, 140, 142
Aviation is highly selective and experienced based, 204
Aviation Maintenance Technicians, 39, 161
Aviation Operations Center, 150
Aviation Operations Team, 146, 147, 148, 170
Aviation organization, xiv, xviii, 1, 3, 4, 15, 16, 24, 27, 29, 30, 31, 35, 36, 37, 38, 40, 43, 49, 72, 73, 74, 75, 85, 86, 88, 89, 90, 92, 93, 94, 95, 98, 101, 106, 108, 109, 110, 114, 115, 127, 132, 134, 136, 138, 139, 140, 144, 145, 146, 147, 149, 161, 163, 164, 172, 179, 180, 187, 189, 190, 192, 203, 207, 210, 211, 213, 215, 221
Aviation Personality Types, 24, 26, 95
Aviation Safety, 5, 6, 7, 8, 12, 13, 38
Aviation Standards Operating Procedures and Manuals, 221
Break areas, 184
budget estimate, 65
cabin crew, 38, 127, 172, 185, 190, 195
Cabin Crew Standards Checks, 190
capital budget, 71
checklists, 8, 172, 189, 196, 197
Checklists, 8
Cleaning an aircraft, 160
Coaching, Counseling and Talking, 25
Common office areas, 184
Communicating the Schedule, 149

communications and education, 75
Compensation, 18, 22, 66, 72
continuous communication, 40
coordinating point, 146
Critical Criteria, 118
Delegation of Authority Tables, 71
Deliberate Decision-Making Process, 80
Department Meetings, 101
determine the right solution, 57
Developing a communications plan, 100
Discretionary or Keyed On Efficiency Types, 136
Dispatch reliability, 130
effective maintenance, 153
Financed acquisition, 141
Financial Audits, 188
financial managers, 64
Financial records, 193
first 90-days, 212
five giant steps, 169
five types of Aviation organizations, 20
Flight Record, 151
Flight records, 193
Flight Standards Checks, 189
four basic components, 15, 16
Fuel and Energy Consumption, 193
Fuel Costs for each type of aircraft, 68
Hearsay, 77
How to get the word out, 100
HR Business Partner, 217
Ice-Breaker, 214
Initial Leaders Discussion Outline, 94
International Standards for Business Aircraft Operations, 188
Leadership award, 210
Leased acquisition, 142
Line Service Technicians, 39, 160
LLC, and Trust entity, 140
London Interbank Offered Rate, 141
Maintaining records, 192
Maintenance Chief, 55, 131, 134, 158, 159, 161

Maintenance record, 193
Mismatches and cultural inadaptability, 91
Mission reliability, 130
mission statement, 1, 2, 3, 4, 5, 16, 23, 35, 51, 61, 86, 87, 92, 177, 213, 220
need four things, 93
Normal mission parameters, 58
Objectives Discussion, 95
Observe the team, 219
organization structure, 215
organizational standard, 37
Outright purchase, 140
Overall Cost, 134
Overall reliability, 130, 155
Quarterly Updates, 50, 106
Routine Communications with Senior Leaders, 84
saboteur, 28, 29, 30
Safety Audits, 12, 189
Safety Awards, 12, 210
Safety Management System, 7, 12, 13, 39
Safety Meetings, 11
Safety Officer, 8, 13, 38, 55, 188
Safety Seminars and Organization, 13
Scheduling, 148, 149
Secured Overnight Financing Rate, 141
Security Audits, 190
security incident, 177
small-team leadership, 29
Special Recognition Award, 210
Specific Mission Briefings, 103
Status Reports, 40, 42
Strategic Objectives, 96
Subordinate Leader Meetings, 55
Tell-Tale Signs, 136
The Hangar, 180
The Mission Package, 150
The organization's wings, 211
Time saving, 170
to support the greater organization, 3, 4, 206

traditional methods, 196
Training records, 193, 218
two primary methods to determine the required budget, 138
Walk the Terrain, 215
Weekly Updates, 41
written policies, 218

Best copilot ever in and out of the cockpit!

Mach .92 at 51,000 feet in a passenger aircraft in a G-600 and before that a Citation X

Presidential Flight Support!

VIP Ski Trip Flight Support

Pilot and Co-Pilot Team

3rd Generation Co-Pilot

www.ingramcontent.com/pod-product-compliance
Lightning Source LLC
Chambersburg PA
CBHW022215090526
44584CB00012BB/558